# Encyclopedia Of Lovebirds
### and other dwarf parrots

### Dr. Matthew M. Vriends

**Pictorial Credits**

*Front and Back Cover:* Horst Mueller
*Black and White:* Dr. Herbert R. Axelrod: 1, 6, 8 (top), 12, 14, 17, 18, 19, 26, 49, 53, 54, 57, 58, 60, 61, 64, 79, 83, 90 (below), 98 (below), 109, 148, 151, 166, 183, 195. Kerry V. Donnelly: 8 (below), 21, 34 (top), 37, 38, 40, 43, 47, 48, 90 (top), 98 (top), 101. Charles R. Fisher: 32. Harry V. Lacey: 29, 136. Miceli Studios: 20, 23, 178. Fred B. Mudditt: 11, 128. Horst Mueller: 145, 209, 218, 226, 235, 238. Louis van der Meid: 42, 50, 97, 99, 199, 223.

ISBN 0-87666-972-0

© 1978 by T.F.H. Publications, Inc. Ltd.

Distributed in the U.S. by T.F.H. Publications, Inc., 211 West Sylvania Avenue, P.O. Box 427, Neptune, N.J. 07753; in England by T.F.H. (Gt. Britain) Ltd., 13 Nutley Lane, Reigate, Surrey; in Canada to the book store and library trade by Clarke, Irwin & Company, Clarwin House, 791 St. Clair Avenue West, Toronto 10, Ontario; in Canada to the pet trade by Rolf C. Hagen Ltd., 3225 Sartelon Street, Montreal 382, Quebec; in Southeast Asia by Y.W. Ong, 9 Lorong 36 Geylang, Singapore 14; in Australia and the South Pacific by Pet Imports Pty. Ltd., P.O. Box 149, Brookvale 2100, N.S.W., Australia; in South Africa by Valiant Publishers (Pty.) Ltd., P.O. Box 78236, Sandton City, 2146, South Africa; Published by T.F.H. Publications, Inc., Ltd., The British Crown Colony of Hong Kong.

# Contents

1. GENERAL REMARKS.....................9
2. BUILDING AND EQUIPPING THE AVIARY...28
   THE FLIGHT: Location; Material; Shape And Size; Layout; Open Section, Covered Section; THE SHELTER: Miscellaneous Considerations; Bird-Room; Inside Aviary; Shrubbery; Maintenance
3. BREEDING POSSIBILITIES...............44
4. THE BREEDING PERIOD.................56
5. THE SEXES............................74
6. CARE OF OUR BIRDS...................86
   Seed; Greens; Fruit; Tree Twigs; Universal Food; Cuttlebone; Drinking And Bath Water; Perches; The Bath; Nest Material; The Floor; The Sick Bird
7. AGAPORNIS CANA.....................112
8. AGAPORNIS PERSONATA FISCHERI......124
9. AGAPORNIS PERSONATA LILIANAE......135
10. AGAPORNIS PERSONATA NIGRIGENIS...141
11. AGAPORNIS PERSONATA PERSONATA....147
12. AGAPORNIS PULLARIA..................159
13. AGAPORNIS ROSEICOLLIS..............174
14. AGAPORNIS SWINDERNIANA............203
15. AGAPORNIS TARANTA..................206

16. *FORPUS* DWARF PARROTS............219
Celestial Parrotlet; Guiana Parrotlet; Delicate Parrotlet; Guyana Dwarf Parrotlet; Hacha Dwarf Parrotlet; Hartlaub's Dwarf Parrotlet; Large-Billed Parrotlet; Ridgeway's Blue-Winged Dwarf Parrotlet or Blue-Winged Dwarf Parrotlet; Spengel's Dwarf Parrotlet; Venezuelan Green-Rumped Parrotlet; Glydenstolpe's Parrotlet; Mexican Parrotlet or Turquoise-Rumped Parrotlet; Sclater's Parrotlet: Spectacled Parrotlet

17. HANGING PARROTS (*LORICULUS* BLYTH)...............................239
Blue-Crowned Hanging Parrot; Ceylon Hanging Parrot; Flores Hanging Parrot; Golden-Fronted Hanging Parrot; Moluccan Hanging Parrot; Philippine Hanging Parrot; Red-Capped Hanging Parrot; Vernal Hanging Parrot; Yellow-Throated Hanging Parrot

18. FIG PARROTS (*OPOPSITTA* SCLATER)....247
Double-Eyed Fig Parrot; Orange-Breasted Fig Parrot

*'Soyons fidèles à nos faiblesses'*
*for Lucy en Tanya*

Colorful lovebirds are fast becoming among the most popular cage or aviary birds available today. Their charming antics, combined with their beautiful plumage, contribute to their widespread acceptance by the avicultural community.

# ACKNOWLEDGMENTS

I am very grateful to the many aviculturists, curators of zoological societies and lovebird enthusiasts who have so generously helped me, in one way or another, in connection with this book, and in particular to those who have so kindly allowed me to use many of their notes on breeding and keeping Agapornidae. In addition to my own experiences and those of friends I have, with the permission of "Cage and Aviary Magazine," Sutton, Surrey, England, consulted E.N.T. Vane's *Guide to Lovebirds and Parrotlets (1959)*.

My grateful thanks are also due to Terry Wiedlewsky for her skilled translations and editing and to Dr. Warren E. Burgess and Jerry G. Walls for their ready help in all matters relating to this book. I should also like to thank Charlene Cavalcante for her invaluable assistance in the preparation of the text. Last but not least, thanks are due to Dr. Herbert R. Axelrod for supplying so many beautiful photographs made especially for this book; in connection with this, I would like to express my special appreciation to Clifton R. Witt of Gaithersburg, Maryland, who very graciously allowed Dr. Axelrod to photograph his beautiful and healthy lovebirds during our recent visit to his breeding establishment—and I'd like to take this opportunity to thank Mr. Witt once again for his very cordial hospitality and all-around friendly helpfulness during our visit. Special thanks to my wife Lucy Vriends-Parent for her assistance and patience; without her this book could never have been written.

All the opinions and conclusions expressed in the following pages are my own, however, and any errors must be my own responsibility.

Neptune, June, 1978 *Dr. Matthew M. Vriends*

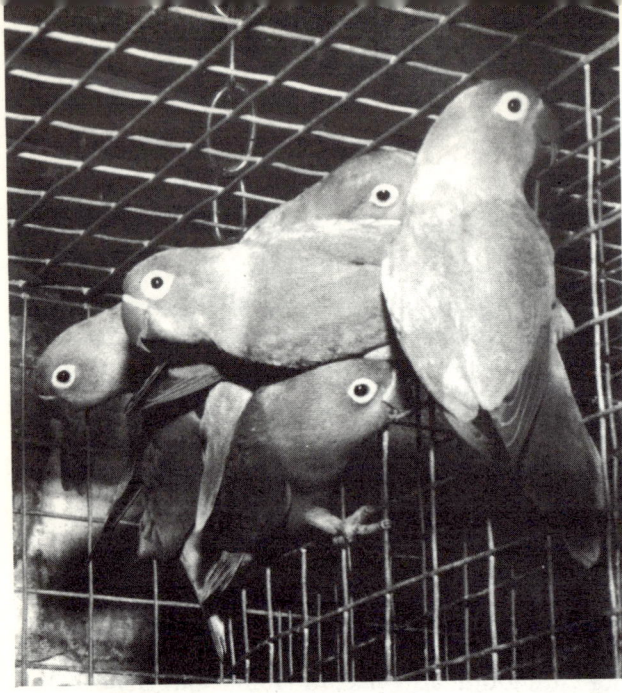

Lovebirds usually live in colonies, which makes them an ideal addition to cage or aviary.

Pictured here is a masked lovebird, just one of the lovebird species available to bird fanciers.

# 1. General Remarks

Lovebirds have become very popular during the past few years. The last ten years have seen an enormous rise in breeding in the United States as well as in South Africa, Australia, Japan and the Netherlands, while England, Germany and Denmark sell thousands of domestically bred lovebirds to pet shops every year.

Lovebirds got their name because of their affectionate natures; the French and Germans, in fact, refer to them as "inseparables" ("Les Inseparables" and "Unzertrennlichen," respectively), although the females of *A. taranta* and *A. cana* are the dominant sex, as they select the nest site and defend this against other birds. They even snap at their mates! Mutual preening of these two species is rather one-sided.

In spite of this, lovebirds are delightful birds, whether kept in a roomy cage or a large aviary. Generally speaking, they breed quite readily and capture one's heart with their adorable chatter. In the wild they often nest in loose colonies, and one tree may shelter many nests.

The genus *Agapornis* Selby belongs to the large group of "noble parrots" (Palaeornidae). Ornithologists recognize approximately 120 different species in the family, several of which are kept as pets in the United States. We will discuss these birds further in a separate chapter.

The genus *Agapornis* is found in the tropical parts of Africa and on the island of Madagascar. *Agapornis* species are recognized by their short, rounded tail. On the average, the birds are about five to six inches (12 to 15 cm) long. Although most of their plumage is green in color, we have recognized species which have some yellow, red and blue feathers. Lovebirds live in small groups in forests, plains and swamps; some species live in mountainous regions up to approximately 3,000 meters above sea level; others still in the open fields, but all species in this genus can be found south of 13 degrees northern latitude.

In the wild the birds feed on various types of grass seeds, sweet berries, fruit, and a variety of grains and grass. In captivity they should be offered a number of different seeds, as well as de-husked oats, rice (including rice that has been soaked in water), berries, millet, new green twigs, egg, melba toast, other fruit such as bananas, orange sections, sweet apple pieces, cherries, pears, raisins and currants (these last two should be soaked), "ant eggs" and the so-called universal mixture. In addition, the birds should be offered cuttlefish bone and oyster grit daily.

A pair of lovebirds will spend the better part of the day together, much of the time on a twig or branch observing the activity all around them in the aviary. Even those lovebirds that enjoy the freedom of the wild will always go to roost in pairs and go off together when searching for food. However, placing various species together in one aviary can lead to some bloody fights; therefore it is advisable to keep different species apart in separate cages or aviaries. With a little luck and a lot of care there are still several possibilities in the area of cross-breeding, as evidenced by some of the successful combinations that have been established over the years. We will come back to cross-breeding possibilities later, but would like to point out now that in no way can cross-breeding be considered a small achievement. It speaks for itself that the crosses listed below are by no means easy to bring about, but possibilities need not be ruled out either! Over the years many successes have been recorded:

Lovebirds are usually found in pairs. A pair of lovebirds will spend a great deal of time together, usually just watching the activity around them. Pictured here is a pair of Fischer's lovebirds.

*A. taranta* x *A. p. personata*, *A. p. fischeri*;
*A. roseicollis* x *A. p. fischeri*, *A. p. personata*, *A. p. lilianae*, *A. p. nigrigenis*;
*A. p. fischeri* x *A. roseicollis*, *A. p. personata*, *A. p. lilianae*, *A. p. nigrigenis*;
*A. p. personata* x *A. roseicollis*, *A. p. fischeri*, *A. p. lilianae*, *A. p. nigrigenis*;
*A. p. nigrigenis* x *A. p. lilianae*, *A. roseicollis*, *A. p. personata*;
*A. p. lilianae* x *A. roseicollis*, *A. p. fischeri*, *A. p. personata*, *A. p. nigrigenis*.

An example of a typical lovebird cage. Most lovebirds can survive in a standard budgerigar cage. For breeding purposes, however, they will require more roomy accommodations, such as a small aviary.

Mr. Ad. Vissers of Drunen (Netherlands) was able to succeed with a crossing of a male *A. roseicollis* and a female *A. personata.* The crossing came about in this manner: Mr. Vissers had a pair of the species *A. roseicollis* and a pair of *A. personata* that were kept in the same cage but were separated by a wire-mesh screen. On a certain day Mr. Vissers noticed that the male *A. roseicollis* was feeding the female *A. personata* through the screen; he immediately brought the two birds together. After a few weeks the first egg was laid, followed by two more. After the normal breeding period, two babies were born, which soon matured beautifully. (Up until this time, the particular crossing of *A. roseicollis* and *A. personata* was not known.) I mention this particular case to illustrate that although various species of birds in the wild are not on friendly terms with each other, they often amaze their owners by being unexpectedly drawn to one another.

Lovebirds live and breed in colonies, although during the breeding period some of them will break away into small groups to share their well and woe together. Even in these smaller groups some disharmony might occur, but to a lesser degree than in the larger colony. In each colony, one of the stronger males will act as leader to intervene successfully if and when little "disagreements" present themselves. This will take place even in an aviary housing several couples of one particular breed. I have observed that these minor arguments are mostly restricted to evening quarrels, for rarely will these birds steal nesting material or food from each other; in any event, their breeding habits are rarely affected by these little upsets.

As a rule, lovebirds lay between four to six eggs each breeding period; in the wild they often lay more. The female plays the larger part in the actual breeding process, her main role being to sit on the eggs until they hatch. At this time the male takes care of feeding her; later he feeds the babies as well! The female certainly takes part in the rearing of the young and often activates the male to do his part in the feeding operation.

It is interesting to note that dwarf parrots differ from all other parrots in that they are rarely or never bred in captivity. In addition, dwarf parrots use nesting materials, while other parrots do not. Lovebirds, in fact, use quite a lot of building materials to construct their nests. Several species even transport these building materials in between their back and/or chest feathers!

There are six full species of lovebirds, all of which are subdivided into a number of subspecies. (It is mostly the coloring and measurements which determine the birds' taxonomic classification.) The male is readily distinguishable from the female in three of these six species: *A. cana, A. pullaria* and *A. taranta.*

Lovebirds are quite popular around the world as aviary birds. Shown here is the Moscow Bird Market.

The above three species are the easiest to keep together in an aviary, and they breed quite readily. They generally rear their young without too many problems. In order to present a total picture of the various species of lovebirds, we will also discuss the species *A. swinderniana*, although this bird is rarely offered for sale in pet shops. In the remaining species of *Agapornis*, the male and female are the same color, which can present problems when one wishes to obtain a pair.

Experience has taught us that birds belonging to the *Agapornis* genus make outstanding breeders, provided that the pairs are indeed pairs (i.e., male and female), they are housed in a roomy aviary with the necessary shrubs for protection, and are offered a balanced diet. It is advisable to exchange one of the birds (preferably the male) should the pair still not breed; in most instances this should take care of the problem. For this reason we strongly urge any breeder to make arrangements with the pet shop to exchange one of the birds in the event that his pair are not male and female. It is noteworthy that the "marriages" made in captivity are generally for life.

The six different species in the genus *Agapornis* include fourteen subspecies, as follows:
1. *Agapornis cana* (Gmelin), subdivided into *A. cana cana* and *A. cana ablectanea* Bangs. Range: Madagascar.
2. *Agapornis pullaria* (Linnaeus), subdivided into *A. pullaria pullaria* and *A. pullaria ugandae* Neumann. Range: West and Central Africa.
3. *Agapornis taranta* (Stanley), subdivided into *A. taranta taranta* and *A. taranta nana* Neumann. Range: southern Eritrea and southwestern Ethiopia.
4. *Agapornis swinderniana* (Kuhl), subdivided into *A. swinderniana swinderniana* and *A. swinderniana*

*zenkeri* Reichenow. Range: Liberia, Cameroon and Congo. (Some recognize yet a third subspecies: *A. swinderniana emini* Neumann).
5. *Agapornis roseicollis* Vieillot, subdivided into *A. roseicollis roseicollis* and *A. roseicollis catumbella* Hall. Range: Southwest Africa.
6. *Agapornis personata*, with four subspecies. *Agapornis personata personata* Reichenow. Range: northeastern section of Tanganyika and southeast of Lake Victoria.
*Agapornis personata fischeri* Reichenow. Range: south and southeast of Lake Victoria.
*Agapornis personata lilianae* Shelley. Range: northern Rhodesia and Nyasaland.
*Agapornis personata nigrigenis* Kirkman. Range: northern section of southern Rhodesia.

We would like to briefly relate the history of these birds, which have really not been known all that long to bird fanciers. It was well over 200 years ago that the *A. cana* (Madagascar lovebird) and *A. pullaria* (red-faced lovebird) were first studied, described and documented. Before that, these birds had not been recognized as separate types. It is not known with any certainty when the first species was imported to Europe for the first time. However, in reading old magazines it would appear that these birds have been making their homes in aviaries and cages in Europe for about a century. According to the available literature on the subject, *A. pullaria* arrived in Europe before *A. cana*, although by only a few years. During the time that they were being imported in such huge numbers, a pair of lovebirds could be bought for only about a dollar. On the Continent they were also selling very cheaply—in Germany for approximately half a mark, and in England for less

Lovebirds are affectionate and will constantly nuzzle and preen their mates. The bonds formed between pairs usually last until one of the partners dies.

than half a crown! Today, of course, the prices are very many times higher, but the true bird fancier will pay the price willingly. In 1882 Dr. Frenzel (Freiburg, Germany) raised some red-faced lovebirds. Two died about three weeks after fledging. In 1886 Dr. H. Adam (Marseilles, France) had two pairs of aviary-bred birds. Mr. C.T. Metzger (Indianapolis, U.S.A.) reared five birds in 1893, out of seven eggs and two clutches.

Although the prices of lovebirds have risen sharply, fanciers are quite willing to pay them for these charming, attractive birds. This is so even in Russia, where this picture was taken.

During the past ten years, the popularity of lovebirds as show birds and as aviary specimens has increased very greatly, as this picture of a Russian bird market illustrates.

In 1860 two Madagascar lovebirds were shown in the Zoological Gardens of London. Shortly afterwards the brothers Hagenbeck (Hamburg, Germany) began importing *A. cana* by the thousands. Dr. K. Russ, the famous German author, bred the first *A. cana* in 1872.

*A. swinderniana* was discovered in the beginning of the 19th century. This particular species has been described countless times in various scientific papers, and judging from some of the old descriptions it would appear that the scientists of that time were quite knowledgeable on the life of this bird. Quite well known, among others, are the studies in "Selby's Parrots" from the *Naturalist Library* of 1836. *A. s. zenkeri* was recognized as a subspecies much later, around the end of the nineteenth century.

In 1814 *A. taranta* was recognized and described, but it was still close to a century later before the first individuals were shipped to Europe. No doubt this can be attributed to the fact that the birds kept in captivity in Africa had practically never bred successfully, so fear existed that the birds to be exported to Europe would perish. The first specimens did, in fact, arrive in England and Germany in deplorable condition. Consequently, attempts at breeding them met with very little success. *A. roseicollis* was discovered in 1793, although

This photo shows the proper way to hold a lovebird in order to inspect the beak and oral area for any visible disorders.

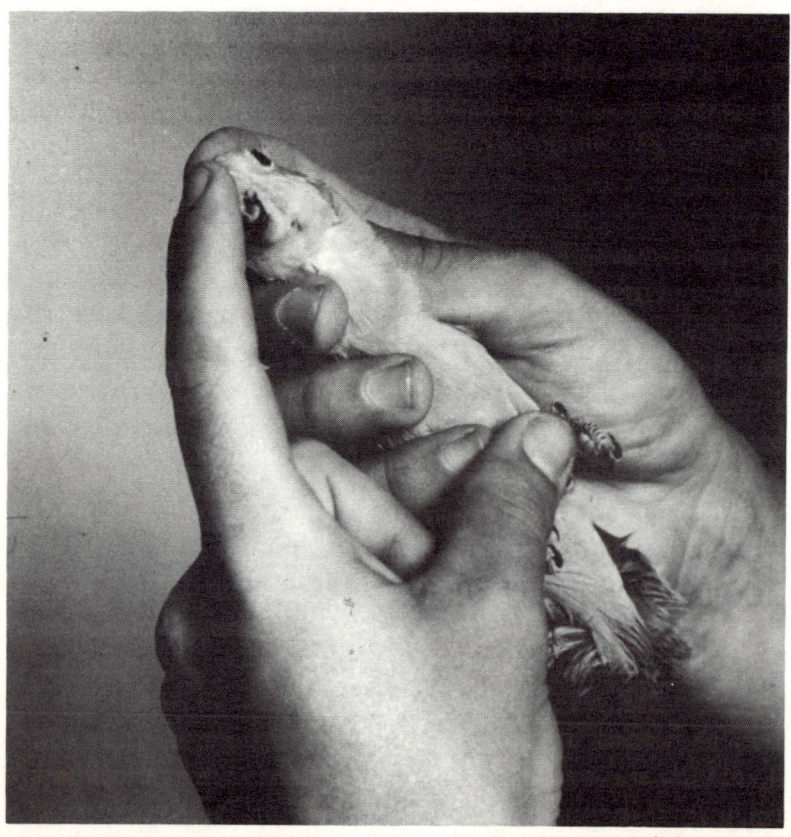

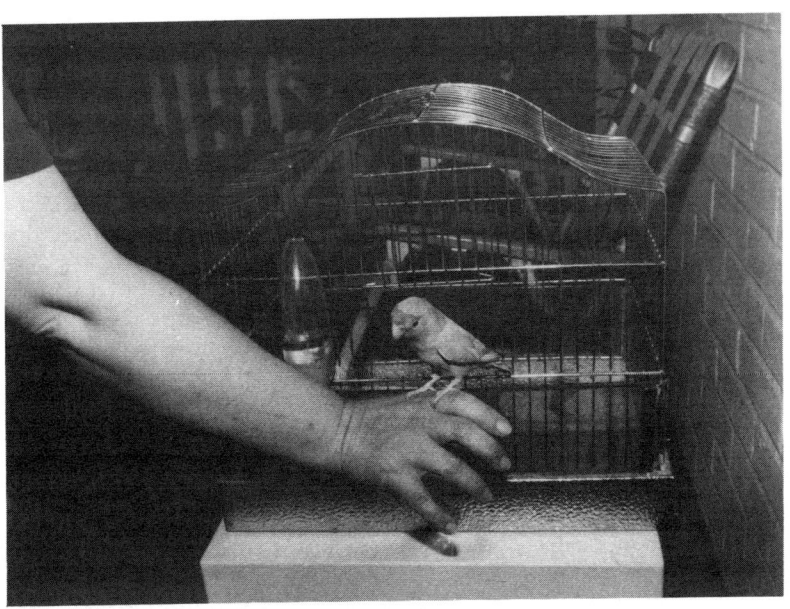

Some lovebirds can be tamed as easily as a budgie, which adds to their desirability as a cage and aviary bird.

it was at first confused with *A. pullaria*. It was not until more than twenty years later, in 1817, that *A. roseicollis* was considered a separate species. The first specimens arrived in England in 1860 and were exhibited in the large London bird show during the same year. A few years later, after this species had proved to be a good breeder, every bird breeder suddenly wanted to own a pair of *A. roseicollis*. Although the demand was greater than the supply, this problem was soon overcome when a few bird breeders put their heads together and decided to share the expensive transportation costs of the birds. Before long there was an abundant supply of good pairs available in England, Germany and Holland. The breeding of these birds continued with such successful results that *A. roseicollis* has long been one of the most popular cage birds in Europe.

In 1908 the first *A. personata nigrigenis* was imported to Europe; it had been discovered only four years earlier, in 1904. Around 1925 *A. personata personata*, *A. personata lilianae* and *A. personata fischeri* came to Europe, immediately receiving a warm welcome from bird fanciers. About this time the grass parakeet also became very popular, especially since some breeders knew how to produce certain colors. Consequently, the popularity of the *Agapornis* genus declined somewhat, although not for long, for the colored parakeets had become so expensive that bird enthusiasts soon turned elsewhere. When the exportation ban took effect, prices of lovebirds soared while the quality of breeding went down. In fact, the state of the dwarf parrot was pitiful indeed: very close inbreeding, half-lame breeders, faulty coloring, malformed birds, etc., if we are to believe the books and magazines prior to 1939. It appeared there was not enough time, material and enthusiasm for breeding really good birds. The lack of enthusiasm was due, of course, to the fact that good lovebirds were simply unavailable. Where could new and pure blood be found for starting a new lineage of top quality birds? And then when World War II came, no doubt there were other priorities. The factories that manufactured bird seed and feeds lay mostly idle. Needless to say, during the war not much was achieved in the area of breeding.

Things changed drastically when the export ban enacted by African governments was lifted. This happened quite unexpectedly, with the result that many breeders began to import as many birds as possible, in a rather unorganized manner and often through fly-by-night bird dealers; many of the birds arrived sick and weak. The natural reaction of the African governments was to reinstitute the export ban. (Considering all these events, it would have been advisable to lift the ban once

Here the relative chestiness of the bird is being inspected to determine whether the bird is underweight or overweight.

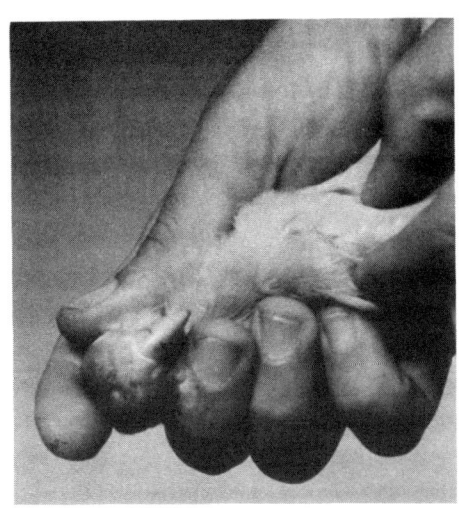

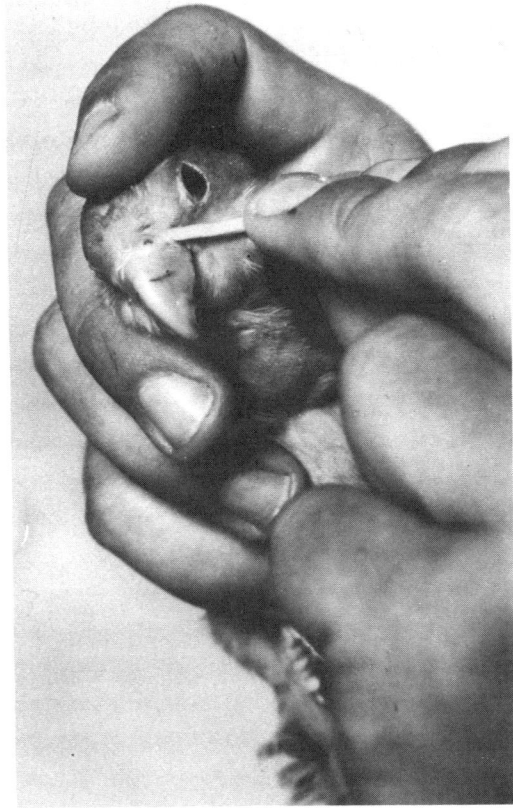

In order to closely examine the nostril area, the feathers surrounding that area must first be pushed back with a blunt toothpick or similar object.

in a while, restricting the number of birds to be captured and exported, and still enabling "new blood" to be introduced on the Continent.) The most important cause for the ban was probably the much feared 'parrot fever' (psittacosis); this danger has been greatly abated by the quarantine procedure currently in effect. Still, the controls that check the enforcement of the ban are not always that effective, as new birds do come in from time to time (although their condition is often questionable), and smuggled birds present special problems. The sale of these birds to retailers also does not always follow correct lines. For example, birds which have not had a chance to become acclimatized are boldly advertised as hardy, healthy birds which "can be placed in an outside aviary without any problems." In practice, this has often proved to be fatal to the life of the birds.

It is sensible to place each bird in quarantine upon its arrival in order to acclimatize it properly; proper nourishment is also recommended. Lovebirds are certainly not difficult birds to keep; indeed, every good bird fancier can successfully keep all varieties of lovebirds. Perhaps quite a few would-be enthusiasts are deterred by claims that dwarf parrots are loud screechers; this is certainly not true! A few varieties tend to be somewhat noisy, but we know of plenty of others that hardly open their beaks.

The nutrition requirements for the birds are not too involved, especially since a large part of their diet is often readily available in the home or garden, and we do not need to rely entirely upon commercial feeds. If we have available the correct nutritional elements and the knack to carefully acclimatize our birds, we can be assured that breeding will take place before too long and that our birds will live long and healthy lives.

By keeping newly-bought birds in a roomy cage or aviary set up indoors (perhaps in a basement, den or attic room), letting them become accustomed to their new diet and waiting some six weeks before taking them outside, the transition to a new environment should be a smooth one. Wait for a warm and sunny day before taking them outside, and make sure that the outside aviary affords a shelter with ample protection from the elements. During the fall, of course, the birds must be brought back indoors. During the winter months, the indoors aviary should not be cold and drafty; some heating will probably be necessary. The acclimatization experiment can be considered successful if the birds have made it through the winter in good shape, and we can feel that our birds are hardy specimens that can stand steadfast against life's little knocks.

Following acclimatization is the subject of breeding. Even if we have our birds breed on a moderate scale, we can be assured that each pair will "pay back" the cost of upkeep. The demand for lovebirds is still greater than the supply, so that we need not have financial worries about the expense of upkeep. However, we cannot overemphasize the importance of not misusing our birds. This would be most damaging to our entire interest in keeping birds, in all of its aspects.

One last point that warrants special attention is that of amateur cross-breeding. Cross-breeding itself is a very interesting branch for the bird fancier; to maintain good birds, however, cross-breeding should only be done with the utmost planning and care. All too often cross-breeding is done in haphazard manner; therefore we strongly advise the amateur bird fancier to leave cross-breeding to the more advanced fanciers, who plan ahead and know exactly how to go about this intricate area of creativity. Hit-or-miss cross-breeding can lead to difficulties, which we will illustrate with a case in point. In California, with its nice suitable weather, fanciers had been enjoying great success in breeding blue *A.*

*p. personata* on a large scale. When this success became known, less serious breeders began to experiment with breeding the blue *nigrigenis*. The final result was that it became impossible to distinguish between the *personata* blue and the *nigrigenis* blue. These two breeds resulted in further cross-breeding, with complete chaos following soon after. The blue *nigrigenis* is beautiful, but when further cross-breeding causes the yellow pigmentation to disappear, *nigrigenis* will look like a twin of the blue *personata*. One will understand, therefore, that crossing different species of lovebirds should be done only after careful consideration. For example, the above mentioned blue lovebirds were heavily bred in Australia, and then sold under the most impressive names and for equally impressive prices!

As bird fanciers, we should do our utmost to prevent any deterioration of the different lovebird species before it is too late.

**Opposite:** Although there are export bans in effect for certain species, there have been so many lovebirds bred domestically that a number of species are still available despite the bans. Shown here is a normal green peach-faced.

# 2. Building and Equipping the Aviary

A good aviary consists of both an outer and inner area, respectively called a flight and a shelter. Let's first talk about the building and equipping of the flight.

## THE FLIGHT

**Location**

Preferably the front of the aviary should face south. If this is not possible, then the front should face as close to south as practicable, choosing southeast rather than southwest. Even if the front of the aviary faces south, part of it should still be made of glass; however, do not use plate glass or something similar. Obviously, a scenic spot with plants, bushes, flowers, etc., that can be seen from the house would be ideal.
Remember that the aviary should be safeguarded against the detrimental effects of the elements, but should be open enough to utilize the beneficial aspects of the environment.

**Material**

It is not advisable to use wood exclusively in the building of an aviary that is meant for lovebirds. Inasmuch as most varieties are known to gnaw, quite a lot of damage would take place before very long. The foundation should be made of concrete. The frame for the sides of the aviary itself should preferably be made of metal, but it can also be made of wood—provided, of course, that if wooden framing is used it should be strengthened and made gnaw-proof by being covered with metal. A brick wall of a foot to one and a half feet

A well constructed aviary will offer an adequate amount of space in which the birds can fly about with relative freedom.

high should be built on the foundation, upon which the floor is then constructed. Concrete would be preferable for the floor, but creosote-soaked railroad ties and other treated wood can also be used; even ceramic tiles would be useful, and are easily kept clean. Asbestos sheets or shingles or similar materials are the best choice for the walls and divisions inside the aviary, since they will be unaffected by any attempts at gnawing.

The roof can also be made of asbestos and would not necessarily require a second covering, although one of roofing tiles would be attractive. The roof should have a slope to allow run-off of rain. If the aviary is built against an existing solid fence, the roof should extend over the fence a little way to prevent rain from accumulating where the fence meets the roof. A strip of asphalt paper can do quite a lot to prevent any water problems. Adding a little gutter would certainly be practical if not entirely necessary.

Shown is another example of an aviary that offers the proper amount of open space and shelter for the birds.

Other materials needed are good quality fine wire netting, metal or iron-wire, nails, and glass. For a half-covered flight area wired glass or shatterproof glass is the best choice. For anyone interested in the construction of outdoor or indoor aviaries for lovebirds and other species, I recommend *Building an Aviary* (Naether and Vriends, T.F.H. Publications).

**Shape and Size**

Since it is advisable to keep just one pair, the aviary need not be especially large. The size of a chicken coop is determined by the number of chickens one plans to keep, but with an aviary for lovebirds it is the other way around: *first* we determine how large we should make the aviary according to available space and location, and then we see how many birds we can keep. If plenty of space is available for the aviary, the breeding of several pairs—even ten pairs—can be considered. In breeding lovebirds, however, space is not the only consideration. Other things have to be taken into account. Climate is just one example: the cooler the climate, the less our chances of successfully breeding lovebirds. (Although some breeders consider the winter season the best period for breeding, we prefer the spring and fall.) Generally, the best results are obtained when we try to breed with just one pair or if we use separate breeding areas when we try with more. (There will be more on this subject under the listing of the various species of lovebirds.)

In any case, the flight should be reasonably longer than the shelter to provide the birds with sufficient space to exercise in. An average guide is to make the flight four-fifths of the entire length of the aviary, although this measurement can be adapted to particular spatial restrictions.

As far as the shape of the aviary is concerned, we would suggest that following straight lines to match those of the aviary's environment will probably be the most suitable. Adding various adornments such as steeples, towers, etc., often renders the aviary odd-looking. The aviary will look best when it blends in with its environment by being situated among bushes, shrubs, and flowers that enhance its appearance. Be sure not to make the aviary too low; the height of the front should be about 6-8 feet.

**Layout**

In general, aviaries consist of three sections: the un-

In a bird-room or inside aviary, a fairly large cage is necessary to allow the birds sufficient room to exercise. In a cage such as this, even breeding is possible.

covered flight, the covered flight and the shelter. If the covered part of the flight is open only at the sides, the nesting boxes could be hung at the back, thus leaving out the shelter altogether. (This may be necessary for reasons of expense or space limitation.) The nesting boxes require a sprinkling with water every day or two during extended dry spells.

Even a free-standing aviary—one which has not been built against an existing fence or garage—can be built without the shelter, by using the nesting boxes as such and hanging them out of view in the backyard. Only the bird keeper would have easy access to them. This type of aviary has much to recommend it, inasmuch as basically it consists of two sections: an open and a covered flight, with the nesting boxes doubling up as the night shelter.

**The Open Section**

Most of the birds that we keep in an aviary cannot spend the winter in the unprotected outer area of the aviary. Therefore it is necessary to either provide the birds with nest boxes or to have a shelter which can be heated by means of a heat-lamp or other mechanism.

For example: in order to give the birds a feeling of freedom, harden them up a little and maintain their colors, they should have access to the completely open section of the aviary. As already noted, this is built mostly of wire netting and metal tubing or wooden beams reinforced with metal strips. Lovebirds and dwarf parrots mercilessly gnaw away at wood. Without some reinforcement then, there would soon be little left of the aviary. As an example, they tear off the bark from trees and shred it into curling fibers which they use in their nesting boxes. Hence our emphasis on using metals, wire, etc., rather than wood. If metal strips and the like are not readily available, we can use fine wire mesh or netting for protection of the woodwork and on any trunks of trees that grow in our aviary.

Even in cages such as these, breeding is possible provided nest boxes are supplied.

This is just a small portion of a large aviary, showing the open section attached to a covered shelter.

**The Covered Section**

This part has a watertight roof and perhaps an asbestos back wall, which separates it from the shelter; the remainder of this section consists of wire netting. The floor can be fashioned of earth covered with sand, although cement slabs covered with sand would be preferable. If concrete or cement slabs are used, the shubbery, of course, will have to be in plant tubs and boxes. Adding fresh willow twigs every once in a while would be much appreciated by your birds.

Naturally, this section must be fitted with several perches. The most common size is ½" in diameter, but it is advisable to vary the sizes somewhat, to allow our birds to pick a perch that is most comfortable for them. They may also like to change their choice from time to time in order to allow their feet a slightly different position, as it can become tiresome for the birds to sit on the same size perch for extended periods of time. More than likely these perches will have to be replaced occasionally, again due, of course, to their enormous urge to gnaw.

Making use of wired glass will prevent the birds from doing damage to themselves, as they are unable to see ordinary glass and will fly head first into it. Plexiglass can also be used, and is certainly less dangerous than glass if a bird should hit it. It is not advisable to hang nesting boxes in the covered section. It is best to keep to this rule: hang the nesting boxes either in the open section or on the back wall where they can be kept wet.

## THE SHELTER

It is highly recommended to have the entrance to the shelter consist of double doors, as this will prevent the birds from flying away. This will allow the bird keeper to enter into a small area, close the door behind him and then enter the second door leading to the flight. Both these doors can be made of wire netting.

The shelter is divided into two parts by means of a shelf-type 'false' floor. The top half is the actual night shelter; the bottom half is vertically split into two parts, one being used as the mating room, quarantine station, punishment room for troublemakers, observation room, etc.; the other part being for storing the nesting boxes, perches, water and food containers, etc.

The floors of both these bottom halves should preferably be made of asbestos, concrete, or tiles; the floor of the actual night shelter should also be made of concrete, but covered with beach sand in a layer approximately 2 to 3 inches thick. The sides of the night shelter are of wire netting, as are those of the inner aviary.

A properly planned shelter includes provisions for adequate ventilation. This usually involves installation of an inlet, placed low and protected against mice, and an outlet on the opposite wall near the eaves.

**Miscellaneous Considerations**

Just a few more remarks about the building of the aviary: when building or pouring the foundation, be sure to bury the wire in the earth as this will help to deter rats and mice; use wire also when pouring the concrete in order to prevent cracks. Make sure the roof is built on a slant and extends to all sides. Use double wire in making partitions. The asbestos may be painted, though this is not necessary. The metal and wire netting can be painted with carbolic acid in green or black, but of course everything must be completely dry before admitting the birds into the aviary. Whitewashing the interior is a waste of time, and dangerous besides, since most of the whitewashes contain some poisonous elements which would be hazardous to our birds, considering the lovebirds' insatiable urge to gnaw.

An additional convenience is electric lighting, both

In an inside aviary, adequate lighting is essential. Here the lights are placed above the cages, far enough away to prevent any damage to the birds, yet close enough to afford the maximum in light. Note that the cages are elevated off the floor to prevent the attack of rodents.

inside and outside of the aviary. When necessary chores must be done on gloomy days or very early in the morning, electric lighting is almost indespensable to the birdkeeper. It is possible to place a powerful light at such a height so as to illuminate an entire group of pens from the top. In this way a bird keeper may easily observe the intrusion of any nocturnal creatures and quickly dispose of them. Electric bulbs within the aviary should always be wrapped with some form of wire screen so that the birds will not come into direct contact with them.

If the birds are ever in full artificial light when it is dark outside, it is necessary to install a dimmer to the circuit. A sudden switch from full light to complete darkness can send birds into such panic that it is quite possible that they may seriously injure themselves.

Finally, keep in mind that a certain amount of extra equipment should be kept on hand, because there will be a certain amount of breakage of materials, and these should be immediately replaced.

Here is another example of the use of electric lighting in an inside aviary.

## Bird-Room

This is really nothing more than an outside aviary constructed indoors, such as in an attic room, basement or any other available space in the house. Construction consists merely of fitting wire screens over the windows, protecting the windowsills, etc. with metal strips and making a little "foyer" by means of an extra wired door to prevent birds from escaping. Four or five mated pairs can breed here, although dividing the available space into small compartments so that each pair has their own "lodging" would be better.

## Inside Aviary

As this is used mostly for keeping and breeding tropical birds, we do not feel that it would be suitable for our purpose. An aviary placed in some living area of the house would not give lovebirds enough room. In addition, considering their nervous dispositions, an inside aviary would be undesirable as the birds would be confined to the aviary regardless of any household disturbances, quarrels, etc. going on. It would be a little different if the aviary were kept in an attic room, for example, where the bird would be undisturbed for the most part. A good idea is to have any inside aviaries placed in a circle so that they all empty out into one flight. Each separate compartment must measure at least 12 x 15 x 22 inches.

Any heated aviary or bird room should always be supplied with plenty of fresh air, or else the birds will become quite listless. Also, if the heated air is deficient in humidity, the feathers of the bird can lose their luster and become dry and brittle. One can easily supply sufficient humidity merely by letting a pan of boiling water evaporate slowly in some obscure part of the aviary where it will not be disturbed.

Maintenance of the aviary is an important consideration. All bird keepers should devote enough time to the upkeep of the aviary to satisfy the sanitary needs of the birds. Shown is an assortment of equipment necessary to the care of the aviary.

## Shrubbery

The main requirements for the health of our birds are air and light. The aviary should be open and as airy as possible, without creating cross-drafts, while the sun should be allowed to shine in freely. Ideal plants and bushes for the aviary are, among others, American or English holly, cedars, common privet, spirea, snowberry, pine and fir species, tamarack, mahogany and hazel.

For the covered area we suggest placing a few dead trees with attractive branch formations; in the uncovered area, small trees and bushes are useful, but hardy plants are preferable. Each year an inspection should be made of the existing shrubbery and the necessary changes and additions to be made. You may ask yourself why not plant only dead trees and compensate by giving the birds lots of greens? There is a reason for this; the shrubbery provides shade as well as edible greens, *both* of which are necessary to ensure the health of our birds.

## Maintenance

At least once a year, the entire structure of the aviary should be thoroughly hosed off; at this time all nesting boxes should be cleaned and/or painted with carbolic acid or disinfectant. (During the winter when we do not breed the birds, we can really take the opportunity to clean the nesting boxes, as these in particular are fertile grounds for disease-producing bacteria and fungi.) In addition, all perches, seed hoppers, water hoppers, bird baths, etc. should be treated with disinfectant. Incidentally, the water and feed hoppers should be placed so that the bird keeper can have easy access to them without causing too much of a ruckus with the birds.

It would be a good idea, if possible, to place the birds in flight cages in order to do a more efficient job in cleaning both the interior and exterior of the aviary, while repairing leaks, filling in cracks, mending the wire netting, checking the gutter, etc. In short, the entire aviary should be brought back into top form! Inasmuch as most lovebirds spend the winter indoors, this large maintenance job can, of course, be done during the winter.

All of the sand on the floors must be replaced and the earth must be turned over and dug up with a spade, although the frequency of this operation depends on the size of the aviary and the number of its inhabitants. The shrubs, which are Nature's perches for our birds, should be pruned while any dying or dead plants can be removed along with any rotting branches, twigs, etc. If we check and repair the aviary every year, hopefully we won't find too many bad "surprises" at any one time. Keep your aviary as clean as possible! Both you and your birds will benefit from it.

In addition to this annual renovation, a regular schedule of maintenance should be observed. One should never allow the interior of the aviary to become

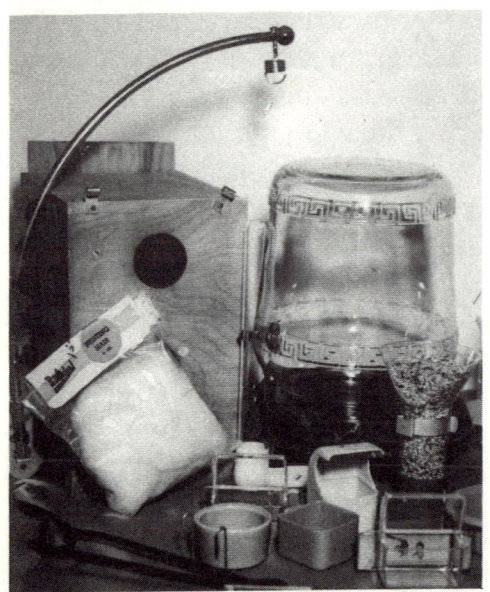

A variety of equipment is available at pet shops for bird keepers to use in the cage or aviary.

Devoted bird keepers will spend many hours with their birds, caring for them and just enjoying them. Pictured is breeder Mr. Clifton R. Witt of The Feather Works, Gaithersburg, Maryland, attending to his birds.

so dirty that it is a disgrace to look upon. It is wise to have a routine so that cleanliness can be maintained. For most fanciers, the weekend is the most convenient time to take care of this essential chore. Remember that one of the primary rules for birdkeeping is to maintain a satisfactorily high standard of cleanliness in the accommodations provided for the birds.

# 3. Breeding Possibilities

As a rule, lovebirds are "valiant" breeders, even though the nesting facilities offered them don't always completely fulfill their needs. This does not mean that lovebirds are very easy to breed and that there are no problems involved in raising the young—it just means that it is entirely possible to get lovebirds to breed and entirely possible to raise a decent number (even if not all) of the young. All in all, it will soon become clear to many readers that breeding lovebirds is no small achievement. But although we'd be the last to claim that breeding lovebirds and other dwarf parrots is a very simple matter, our experience has proved that we can count on success if we stick to the standard guidelines for breeding and care.

The first requirement for breeding lovebirds, assuming that both sexes are represented in your breeding stock, is that the number of nesting boxes should exceed the number of mated pairs. It may sound strange, but lovebirds won't breed unless they have a more adequate choice of nesting areas. There is a lot of controversy surrounding this subject, and a reader of all of the conflicting accounts about breeding lovebirds published in avicultural magazines can soon become almost completely confused.

In order to achieve good final results, we recommend the following specifications for nesting boxes, which we personally find to be the best after having experimented with various kinds for several years.

We began by assuming that the nesting boxes should be roomy and easily kept moist. This business of keeping the boxes moist is very important; in those that are too dry the young birds still within the egg will dry up. Keeping them too wet is equally bad; moderation is the key word. The diet of the parents is also extremely important in assuring the success of the brood. If the recommended dosage of vitamins is lacking, the eggs will not possess the vitality necessary to survive, and several of them will probably not be fertilized. (More on this subject when we talk about the care of lovebirds and other dwarf parrots.)

Minerals are important for the proper breeding of lovebirds. There are many ways in which to assure that your pet gets a sufficient amount of minerals in his diet. Ask your pet dealer for information and advice.

Minerals are also very important. If we give our birds a proper diet they, in turn, will tend to pay more attention to the nesting boxes by keeping them moist, turning over the eggs regularly, etc., which will result in less upkeep for us. Nothing is better for the birds than to leave as much as possible to Mother Nature. Birds that are in excellent health will, for example, wet the nesting materials in the bird bath or water dishes before taking them to their nests. Again, the proper amount of moisture plays a very important part in the success of a clutch; for this reason we hang up our nesting boxes where they will not be in a direct line with the sun's rays. Another method, previously brought up in the chapter on building aviaries, is to hang the nesting boxes on the back wall so that they can be checked by the bird keeper without entering the aviary and disturbing the birds. The ideal spot, therefore, is where the rain will readily wet them, but where the sun's rays are somewhat restricted.

Naturally it is important that we have easy access to the nesting boxes without upsetting the females on the eggs. As lovebirds are very nervous and susceptible to shock, it is important that we not look inside the nesting box when the female is sitting on the eggs. Caution is the key word here. Even when the female is away from the nest we should still proceed with care. During the breeding season especially the birds have a tendency to be easily startled; they may fly with force against the wire or try to hide in a corner, screaming all the while. It can take quite some time then before peace is restored, and naturally such upsets are anything but good for the success of the clutch. Birds that have been recently imported (such as from Japan) are particularly jumpy in contrast with those that have been aviary-bred for generations; the latter are certainly less inclined towards nervousness, and checking on them is not nearly as risky.

Instituting these checks is necessary inasmuch as the chicks have to be ringed when they are about five days old. Ringing procedures require a lot of caution too, since many of the females will do all they can to remove the rings from their chicks' feet. This can result in some very unfortunate consequences, such as a chick falling out of the nest and, if not killed by the fall, then perhaps lying on the ground with a broken or badly wounded leg. Personally we feel that we can do without placing the ring on the fledgling's foot, but on the other hand, lovebirds without a ring cannot take part in bird shows. The bird fancier who is satisfied with the breeding of lovebirds as a hobby can forget about the ringing procedure. By keeping detailed records we can keep track of our birds and their clutches just as well, without needing the rings for identification. However, fanciers who are very much into shows will need to place the rings on the chicks, and should take much care in doing so.

The bird keeper must be sure that he has more nest boxes than he has pairs of lovebirds, because the birds will breed better if they have more of a choice of a nesting site than if only one is provided.

If the bird fancier wishes to make nest inspections, it is advisable to hang the nest boxes on the outside of the enclosure, thus affording the fancier easy access to the nest box while leaving the birds relatively undisturbed.

**Opposite:** When the right conditions are in effect, even amateur breeders can produce results such as this beautiful bird.

If after one week following the ringing procedure nothing has happened, we can safely assume that the parents have not been bothered by them, and that in all likelihood they will not unwittingly endanger their chicks in a last attempt to remove them. Blackening the rings by holding them in the flame of a candle will often help to avoid parental intervention for it is particularly the bright, shiny (and strange) nature of the object that so annoys the parents. Apparently it does not occur to the parents that in removing a newly-placed ring they may finish by killing their offspring.

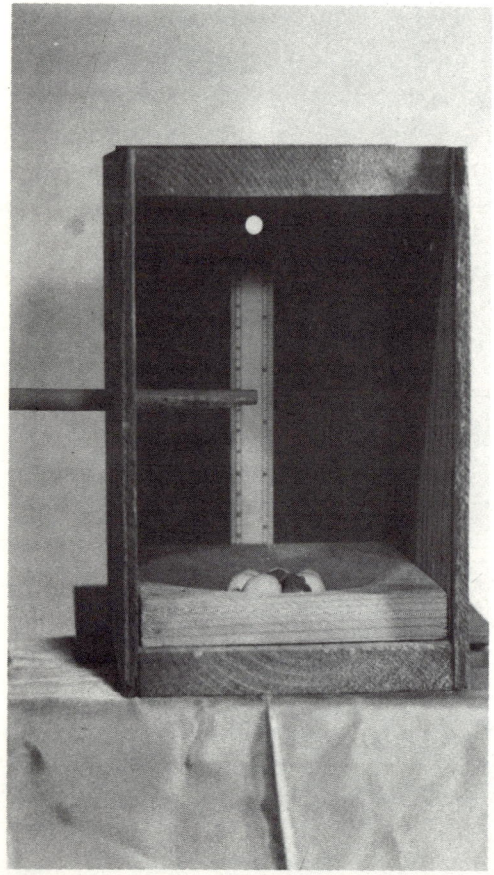

Pictured here is a standard nest box for a pair of lovebirds. It closely resembles the nest box of the budgerigar

The lovebird varieties that have pronounced circled markings around the eyes use very fine grass, roots, etc. for their nesting materials. *A. roseicollis*, for example, builds a fairly open nest without attaching the little "dome" for protection. The other species of lovebirds that have rings around the eyes build sturdier nests of twigs and roots, some even using leaves as building materials. Understand that any interference on your part—such as moving the nest with one hand in order to get a better look at it—will not go unnoticed by the female; she might become very nervous indeed and leave the nest, possibly for good!

Many species of lovebirds like to use the stalk of spraymillet and the blades of long grass. When there is ample building material available for the birds (such as the bark of willow, oak, beech, hazel, or elderberry trees) they will often build a two-story dwelling: a "sitting room" below and a little "hall" above. Sometimes this little hall is partially hidden in one of the sides. The birds do spend some time in this hall, but the actual purpose of it has not yet become clear to ornithologists. We have observed that the construction of this little compartment is usually finished after the nest itself has been completed. Perhaps this little hall serves as an occasional sleeping compartment for the male and later for the chicks, but the female spends some time there too, even after the eggs have been laid. The chicks and particularly the male sleep on the roof of the nesting boxes when the female has started to brood again. As you can see, there is still a lot we do not know about these dwarf parrots. . . which constitutes another excellent reason for keeping them!

In the beginning of this chapter we stated that the nesting box should not be too small. Ideal measurements are 8 x 8 x 10 inches deep. As you can see, this closely resembles the nesting box of the budgerigar. With a larger box there is a good chance that the birds will not or cannot adequately build the nest, so that some eggs may become lost or damaged. Hardwood is used for the construction of the boxes; oak or beech of about an inch thick is preferable.

The box opening should not be too big, since this will give the birds a feeling of insecurity. More than once, bird breeders have found that when the openings are too big, large birds will inspect the nesting boxes and instigate fierce fights which are often at the expense of the brood. Should the opening be too small, the lovebirds will most likely remedy the situation themselves. However, to eliminate any problems, we would recommend the box opening for the small lovebirds to be 2 inches in diameter and 2½ inches for the large lovebirds. Sometimes the birds will make the original hole smaller from the inside by piling up nesting material

This entrance hole has been the subject of many debates among breeders of this type of bird. It is frequently pointed out that the direction in which the entrance hole faces is significant and that nest boxes in the northern hemisphere will benefit by having a north-facing entrance hole. However, it is my opinion that it is not so much the geographical location of the opening but the presence or absence of light that has so much bearing upon the breeding habits of the hens. In my own experiments, I have found that smaller entrances seem to be preferred by these birds. A smaller hole permits less light to enter the box. It is obvious that a more diminutive opening facing the north would allow only a minimum of light to enter the nest box. Therefore, it seems fairly logical to conclude that it is the lack of light inside the box, and not the geographical positioning of the entrance hole, that is influential in the successful breeding of these birds.

Lovebirds without the ring around the eye have

The ideal size for the opening of the nest box should be just large enough for the bird to get in and out. A larger opening will make the bird feel insecure and will only get filled in by the bird later.

slightly different nest-building habits. They tend to use softer buildings materials such as turf, damp peat, and leaves; on this soft little bed they lay their eggs. It is helpful to place some turf on the bottom of the box so that the birds can easily take some of this material to add to and fashion their nests. The nesting boxes for these species are considerably larger. Boxes that are 12 x 18 x 12 inches deep have proved to be the most suitable. Again, the opening should not be too large; a diameter of 2½ inches would be adequate.

Another important consideration to make in preparing the nest box is the incorporation of a substantial ladder. Wildmesh and wire netting are both excellent building materials for the construction of this ladder. Place the ladder far enough away from the surface to allow sufficient room for the bill and feet of the climbing bird to grasp the "rungs" of the ladder. Bear in mind that the chicks will eventually have to climb out of the nest and any instability will hinder their progress.

Lovebirds having the pronounced eye ring around the eye, such as the masked lovebird pictured below, build nests not having the dome attachment common to the nests of lovebirds that don't have the eyering.

We should construct a small perch (about two inches long) about three-quarters of an inch down from the opening. Be sure that there are a few little holes in the bottom of the box for drainage, in order to efficiently regulate the humidity. A dish of water or a wet sponge is suitable for this. Every box has a double bottom; the one for the eggs of course should also have several small holes in order for the humidity between the two floors to reach the eggs. Once the chicks have flown from the nest for the first time, it is possible that (a few days later, quite suddenly) the mother may no longer feed them sufficiently for the simple reason that she has started on a new brood. As a rule, the male can take over the feeding of the chicks well enough on his own, but if this should not prove to be the case, we will have to feed them by hand. This seems to us to be a better alternative than attempting to hand them over to foster parents.

For the first few nights the fledglings will continue to disappear into the nesting box, even though the female may be sitting on new eggs. This does not constitute any cause for concern.

There are cases where the female has already laid one or two new eggs while the fledglings of the previous brood have not even flown from the nest. If the aviary is constructed with double wire, including the roof of the open section, there is no reason why the nesting boxes should not be hung just a little lower than the roof so that dad and his brood can sleep on top of the box. However, if the wire is just one single layer, do not hang the boxes that way as the birds will then be easy prey for cats, rodents, etc.

# 4. The Breeding Period

Although the chapters to follow will cover the methods in which the various species of lovebirds may be stimulated during the breeding period, we wish to make some important notations at this point. After all, for most hobbyists breeding is the most important and interesting part of their hobby.

Although breeding lovebirds years ago was considered an impossibility, the last decade has produced a number of prominent bird breeders who have proved the opposite to be true. There have been countless enthusiastic articles written by breeders of lovebirds and other dwarf parrots in recent years. When we wrote this book, we received advice from various bird fanciers who exchanged and discussed their ideas and breeding techniques with us. It was unanimously agreed that although breeding dwarf parrots is fairly complicated, it certainly can be done, provided we have excellent bird keeping facilities and offer a well-balanced diet to our birds. This does not guarantee free sailing each and every time, or that unforeseen and unexpected difficulties will not arise. However, determination should eventually lead to success, and the experienced bird fancier hopefully will have his hobby generate extra income for him as well.

The breeding procedure of lovebirds is most interesting and remarkable. Many of their actions are peculiar only to lovebirds, having rarely been noted in the breeding habits of other bird species. There are species of lovebirds, for example, where the female places nest material she has gathered between her feathers and transports it in that fashion to the nursery, rather than in her beak. Seldom does the male participate in the gathering of nest material; at the most he may make minor adjustments in the building of the nest.

There have even been cases where, in a suitable environment, mature hens have laid a clutch of eggs without the aid of a partner. Ordinarily, the normal behavior of a courting male bird is sufficient stimulus for the female to breed. This particular trait, in conjunction with the fact that the hen will start spending periods of time within the dark interior of the nest, causes the hen to ovulate. It is possible for a hen in captivity to rear her family without any aid from the male, however, it is a rather demanding responsibility.

Lovebird hens usually lay a clutch of about five eggs; shown here is an average clutch. Lovebirds cannot be encouraged to lay more eggs by removing eggs from the nest as they are laid.

Occasionally, two lovebirds of the same sex will act as a pair, and some will even go so far as to begin the nesting procedure. These homosexual attachments usually do not last long and are usually dissolved when a more suitable partner is found.

With most lovebirds this is not the case; the female starts to sit on the eggs when two or three have been laid; the male takes care of feeding her; later he helps with the rearing of the young, even after they have first flown out of the nest. For a short period after the fledglings have first flown out, they will still spend the night in the nest.

Eggs are ordinarily laid at two-day intervals. The length of these intervals can be altered, however; cold weather and poor nutrition will lengthen the intervals, while good food and warm weather will shorten them.

According to the age of the hen, the species of bird, and the quality of the food, the size of the clutch can and usually will vary. A young hen may lay only one egg, while most adults lay clutches of two. Sometimes the first egg laid will cause incubation to begin, but this process is normally postponed until the clutch nears its completion. Cold weather can lengthen the incubation period, but it cannot be abbreviated below a certain time.

Approximately two days before the chick is ready to hatch, it can be heard cheeping within the egg. Also, at about the same time, one can detect the slight tapping made by the beak as it strikes against the shell in the process of hatching. During this process, the chick rotates the shell around its body in an effort to escape. The chick's egg-tooth will cut through the shell at the larger portion of the egg. One should, however, resist the temptation to try to assist a chick in its escape from the egg. It has been discovered that premature removal of the chick from the egg could cause hemorrhage due to the ruptured blood vessels of the "shell membrane." This extreme loss of fluid will prove fatal to the chick. A complication arises when the yolk-sac is not taken into the chick's body, a process that usually takes place during a normal, uninterrupted hatching period. This explains why chicks will almost invariably die within a day. Conversely, if a chick has not hatched within two days of the audible cheeping, it will also expire. This is due, in part, to the exhaustion of the chick which results from the struggle of hatching. Another reason is the ultimate increase of harmful metabolites in the tissues, and, finally, due to dehydration. Dead-in-shell chicks

Pictured are peach-faced chicks. The chicks above are 8 and 12 days old respectively. Below is pictured a chick at the age of 15 days.

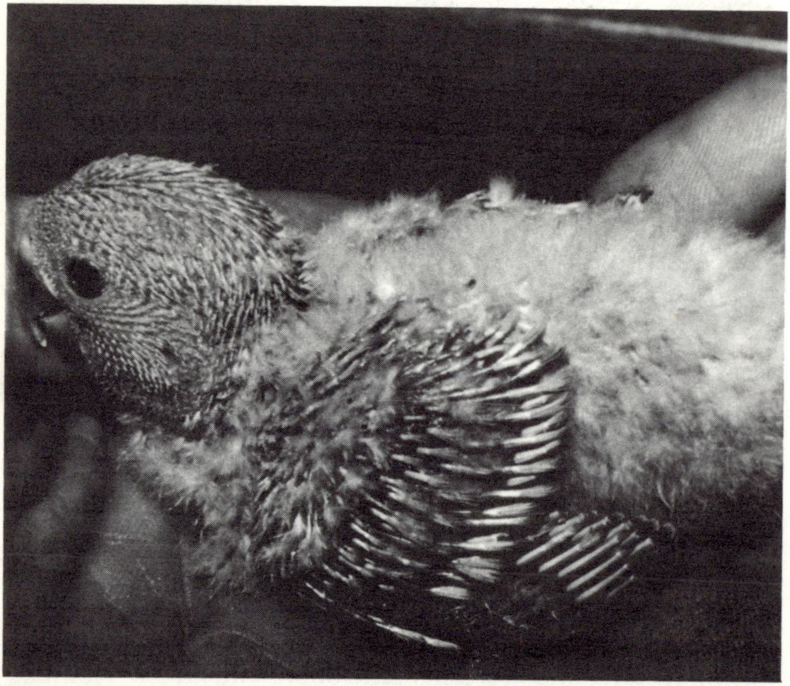

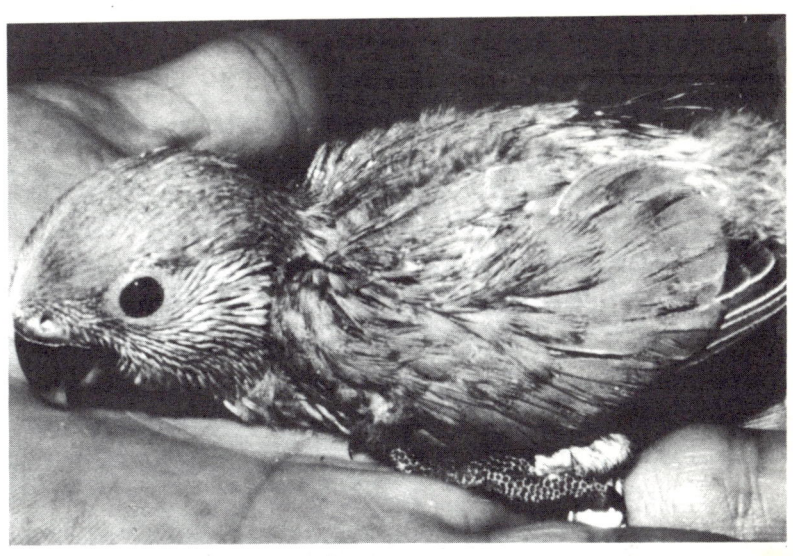

The peach-faced chick above is 25 days old, and the one below is 27 days old.

are often found to be waterlogged and the eggs have a greater weight than those that hatch. An extremely cool or damp atmosphere is usually reported to be the cause of these deaths.

The limbs of a newly-hatched chick are usually extremely weak, but the will to survive is so great, that as soon as the head is free of the shell, the chick will quickly get the rest of its body out of the shell as well.

To cut down on the risk of losing a brood, we advise breeders to allow just two or at the most three clutches per year per pair. The best time for breeding is from April to mid-September. It is advisable to separate the older birds during the winter season, in order to prevent breeding. Not separating the birds would be to promote extreme inbreeding and the premature laying of eggs. We know of females that began to lay eggs at the tender age of four months! This is much too young for the bird; it is advisable to only breed birds that are at least 14 months old. Otherwise we can expect unfertilized eggs, prematurely laid eggs, stillborn chicks, etc. Watch out for too much inbreeding. This can best be avoided by swapping some of your birds with another fancier now and then, thereby obtaining new blood in your flock. These precautions will help you achieve success with your hobby.

Experience has taught me that lovebirds are fertile for a great many years. I have known of cases where birds that were ten or eleven years old were still successfully breeding and rearing offspring. You can see that with proper care a good couple can give you years of enjoyment.

Once again I would like to advise readers to bypass the nest inspections if possible, unless the nesting boxes are built and hung up in such a manner that the inspections can take place without upsetting the birds. Birds that have lived in aviaries for several generations, of course, tend to stand up to the harassment of these inspections better than recently imported ones which are not yet accustomed to aviary life. For those birds that have not yet acclimatized, nest inspections can prove to be fatal due to shock. We must add, however that lovebirds and other dwarf parrots are creatures of habit; if we start nest inspections with aviary-seasoned birds we should continue to repeat them. In other words, either make inspections on a regular basis or do not make them at all; it is my own opinion that the latter is the better choice with us.

Experience has also shown that our birds will be much more at ease with us if we make a habit of talking out loud to them or singing the same tune each time we approach the aviary. In a few days your voice will be a sign to your birds that you are approaching and as time goes by you may notice that they are not disquieted by the presence of their keeper.

Keep in mind that during the breeding season especially, the birds need fresh fruit and greens in addition to their normal daily diet. The green algae that often forms around the edge of the water dishes can be eaten by the birds—in fact, they seem to enjoy it, and it does seem to do them some good.

Although there is a difference of opinion regarding the issue, I feel it is not necessary to clear the nesting boxes between the first and second clutches. This simply scares off the birds, who will usually use the same box the second time around. After the second or even the third clutch, of course, it becomes necessary to clean and disinfect the nesting boxes.

It is sometimes wise to remove hatched egg shells from the nest, for they can frequently wrap around the remaining unhatched eggs, preventing these chicks from breaking out of the egg shell. Unhatched eggs can be left in the nest for about a week to provide extra warmth for

One should remember not to place lovebird chicks of one species into the aviary of another species, as the older birds will kill younger members of another species who try to beg food from them. Note the lovebirds pictured above—they are all masked lovebirds.

the newborn chicks.

Frequently the female will start on the next brood before the last of her chicks has left the 'maternity-room.' In such a case there must be a second nesting box where the chicks can spend the nights after the female will no longer have them in her nesting box. It is important that the bird keeper make sure that the male is providing an ample supply of food for his offspring. At this point however, it is typical for the youngsters to help themselves to millet. Once they have become independent of their parents they must be separated and placed in another aviary. Even in their new surroundings there must be nesting boxes hung up, because for a while longer the young birds will spend their nights in these boxes.

The black masked lovebird is easily cross-bred with other dwarf parrots, making it difficult to buy pure-bred masked lovebirds. Photo by Dr. Herbert R. Axelrod.

Catching these young birds is quite a simple task if it is done when they are asleep in the nest. One must be sure that neither of the parents is in the box. Remove the nesting box and its contents to the new abode, keeping the opening of the box closed by means of a little door. Naturally, there must be ventilation holes in the box. The next morning you can return the box to the parents, who on the whole, will not seem to be perturbed that their brood is no longer in it. Make sure you do not place the chicks in an aviary next to that containing the parents. Neither should you place them with other lovebirds nor with any other species, as the chicks may beg food from the older birds, who will make no bones about killing these "pests."

As previously stated, we are not advocates of ringing the birds. Plastic rings will be gnawed until they are broken, while metal rings often result in broken or wounded feet or legs. If the parents are unable to remove the rings they simply throw them out of the nest, not realizing that there is a baby bird attached to the offending object! Sometimes sturdy rings are attached so tightly that they interfere with the blood circulation in the feet; the foot will soon die if the ring is not quickly removed.

Hens will intentionally seek out their offspring by using the cries of the baby birds to direct them. The thin, high cry of the very young chick is more appealing to the hen than the harsher, more robust calls of the older offspring. This serves to balance out the physical inequalities between the older, stronger chicks, and the weak, newly-hatched ones, and assures that all chicks are satisfactorily fed.

Hens do not always instinctively recognize the cries of their own offspring. This knowledge is acquired through the experience of actually caring for their chicks. Once they learn the cries, however, they become extremely perceptive to only those cries and are incapable of answering the cries of any chick whose voice does not match the one they are accustomed to. Because of this, hens are quite attentive to the needs of their young. If they were not, all of the chicks would starve, because they are totally unable to feed themselves and are quite dependent upon a response to their cries.

Lovebirds can be divided into two groups according to the color of the down of their fresh-hatched progeny. Sexually-dimorphic lovebirds (redfaced, Madagascar and Abyssinian) produce chicks that are covered with white down, and sexually monomorphic lovebirds (peach-faced, and the white-eye-ringed forms) have chicks covered with red down. Since, in the darkness of the nest, these colors would be indistinguishable, one could safely assume that the color of a chick's down would be irrelevant to the hen. Dilger discovered that hens that had never had any previous experience with chicks would accept chicks of an "incorrect" down color. Experienced hens, however, would not accept chicks of another down color. Since down color made no difference to the inexperienced hens, one must presume that the experienced hens responded to the cries of the young and not their color.

It may happen for reasons not clear that the parents will stop taking care of their chicks before they have had the chance to mature a bit. In such a case the bird keeper will have to rear the chicks himself. There have been cases where the chicks were deserted by their parents at the age of three or four days, yet were successfully reared by the bird keeper.

Place the chicks in a warm area of about 90°F (32°C) and hand-feed them every two hours. Their food must be soft and thin, but later, when they are about one week old, the consistency of the food can be a little thicker. Inspect their crops often, and if they are filled

The red-headed lovebird (left) builds its nest in the nests of termites. Abyssinian lovebirds (below) are friendly little birds and are fairly easy to tame. Photos by Horst Mueller.

Masked lovebirds are real seedeaters and should be supplied with a wide variety of seeds. Photo by Paul Kwast.

at regular intervals, the fledglings should make good progress.

The crops should never be completely empty; if the two hour pauses between the feedings are too short, make the adjustment accordingly. If the intervals are too long, shorten the timespan between feedings. It is quite simple to ascertain if the crop is almost empty or not, as the birds are quite naked. They are easy to handle, and each inspection can be easily executed. The little down that they do possess does not count for much!

The temperature of the food should be hand-warm and should remain warm during the feeding. Placing the food in a dish with warm water will maintain a constant temperature. A baby dish with a warm water compartment is even more convenient for feeding the fledglings, and if you want to go all out for convenience, there are electrically heated baby dishes available in the stores.

A plastic eye dropper can be an excellent tool for feeding the fledglings. In the beginning it will be necessary to hold the beak open with the nails of your thumb and index finger, but soon enough the young bird will learn to open his beak by himself.

At feeding time place the baby bird on a heated towel on top of the table and proceed with the feeding operation; afterward, cleanse the beak with lukewarm water. (The towel will need to be washed frequently, as the fledgling will soil it often.)

The fledlglings' food should consist—according to E.N.T. Vane and L. Vriends-Parent—of a thin porridge of baby cereal, peanut butter, honey, cane sugar, a few drops of cod liver oil, cooked oatmeal, and after about a week, soaked brown bread. The bread can be soaked in either water or milk, though milk would be more nutritious. Soon the birds will eat soaked millet and later unsoaked millet. After about a month, the little creatures will become independent.

After the first few days, the growth of the chicks should be continuous. They may, however, lose weight if subjected to cold, damp weather. Regularly weighing chicks and plotting a graph of their weights not only helps to anticipate the chick's expected growth rate, but also helps to prevent serious problems. Seeing a downward slope to a weight chart should warn the serious breeder that something is amiss and steps should be taken to alleviate the problem.

Generally, the chicks will open their eyes on or about the tenth day. The secondary down follicles, which have been growing since about the fourth day, will now start to show their gray down. Shortly, the feather follicles begin growing, and the chick's body weight starts slowing down once the first feathers break. A few days after the appearance of the feather colors, the chicks will begin to leave the nest.

The Madagascar lovebird has no ring around the eye and has the smallest beak of all lovebirds. Photo by Horst Mueller.

The upper bird at right is a vernal hanging parrot; the lower bird is a blue-crowned hanging parrot. So named for their ability to sleep hanging upside down, these brightly colored dwarf parrots are quite popular with bird fanciers throughout the world. Photos by Horst Mueller.

Pictured at right is a black-collared or Swindern's lovebird, a species rare in captivity. Below are golden cherry lovebirds, a mutation of the peach-faced. Photos by Horst Mueller.

# 5. The Sexes

One of the biggest problems for the bird fancier is to be able to distinguish between the sexes. We will discuss a few methods here, though none of them is 100% foolproof. The pelvic bone test seems to offer the best chances for success, but we will add a few other methods so that the bird fancier can choose the method he is most comfortable with.

*A. pullaria*, *A. cana* and *A. taranta* will certainly not give any difficulties in this regard. This is not the case, however, with the lovebird species that have the pronounced ring around the eye, nor is it the case with *A. roseicollis*, where only the laying of an egg gives 100% certainty as to the sex of the bird!

Some experts feel that the female has a slimmer build than the male, but others have claimed the opposite to be true. One would have to be quite an expert to distinguish between the sexes in these species, and we tend to doubt that anyone can do this! The brighter colors of the male are not dominant enough to tip the scale towards that method, as different birds of the same species but from another region (or bred in a different aviary) are not always exactly the same shade of color. Besides, after a while the brighter colors viewed in the aviary appear to fade somewhat and all the birds take on an identical appearance. It is important, therefore, that we find a method not linked with outer appearance that will help us to differentiate between the male and female lovebirds.

Supposedly, the young *A. p. lilianae* and *A. p. nigrigenis* can be distinguished by the color of the iris, as reportedly proved in tests performed by the Marquis of Tavistock. However, we accept this theory with reservations since we have found that the color of the iris is the same or becomes the same in young birds. Mr. Vane, on the other hand, suggests making nesting boxes available to young lovebirds immediately after they have become independent and moved to a separate aviary. If two birds start building a nest together, we have positive proof that we have two different sexes at work. We find the virtue of this method somewhat questionable, since it is not impossible that fertilization may take place with females suffering from premature egg-laying or extreme inbreeding. Of course we will have determined their respective sexes, but by a rather risky means.

By evening we would have to transfer the young pair (and I shudder as I use the word "pair") to a separate aviary, and this can be difficult, too. A small door would be needed to cover the opening of the nesting box, which we would move just before dusk. Of course the birds would not be allowed to leave the box until the next morning. This is quite a troublesome method, and certainly not one without danger. Our birds could suffer shock from all this, and then where would we be?

It is a well-known fact that the female sleeps inside the box most of the time, while the male sleeps on top of it. By applying a little paint to the bottom of the opening of the nesting box we could determine the sexes of the birds since the bird with paint on the feet would have to be the female. (Of course, only a lead-free paint should be used.) Even this method is not all that trustworthy, however, since the male ventures into the box now and then, either to take a peek or to make some nest adjustment.

There remains the pelvic-bone test, which is also not 100% accurate, but we feel this method is by far the best. With young lovebirds this test is quite difficult to perform but that should not matter since the birds should not be used for breeding until they are about

Madagascar lovebirds are successful breeders only when left to themselves, unlike the Fischer's lovebird (opposite) which does not mind nest inspections. Photos by Dr. Matthew M. Vriends (above) and Horst Mueller (opposite).

fourteen months old anyway. This test can be performed on birds that are between four and eight months old; after all, we can only use the means that are available to us. Good suggestions from bird breeders with regard to a better method are always welcome.

Adult males have a fairly wide pelvic bone measurement, but generally the females are broader. Females that have already laid eggs have a larger opening between the pelvic bones than those that have not. A bird with pelvic bones that practically touch each other is almost certainly a male. If one can place a thumb between these bones, then we are dealing with a female.

This method is easiest to perform on *A. roseicollis*, while *A. personata* is most difficult to work with. It is highly recommended that we obtain the option to exchange one of our birds in the event that it should prove to be the opposite of the sex we desire.

How do we perform this test? It is known that lovebirds should be handled as little as possible since they are easily thrown into a state of shock. With this test however, it is necessary that the bird be held in both hands. The thumb should rest on the shoulders of your bird. People who are left-handed should use the right thumb. The right thumb should then be placed in the area of the pelvic bones. If we feel that the two "points" are fairly far apart, then our bird is a female.

Another method of determining the sex of your lovebirds is by observing the manner in which they hold their tail feathers. Mr. H.H. Jacobsen discovered that the hen lovebird is apt to communicate her sexual dominance by slightly flaring her tail. The males, on the other hand, physically defer to their mates by contracting their tail feathers and holding them together more tightly. This is a constant behavioral characteristic of lovebird society; however, the results gained by this process are not always conclusive. Other factors must be taken into consideration. A dominant bird may be in a temporary state of fear caused by the intrusion of the observer, and will contract the tail feathers, holding them in the position of a more submissive bird. Or, conversely, a subservient bird may defensively fluff his tail feathers, appearing, for all intents and purposes, to be the more assertive of the birds. Then too, regardless of sex, when two individual birds have shared living quarters for some period of time, their own distinct personalities will render one aggressive and the other passive. This method, however, can be used in conjunction with others in determining the sex of a bird.

Determining the sex of your lovebird is generally quite difficult. It is virtually impossible, from outward appearances alone, to tell the males from the females shown in this photo, for example.

The Philippine hanging parrot, pictured on these two pages, is generally a healthy bird and usually becomes acclimatized rather easily. Photos by Dr. Matthew M. Vriends and Horst Mueller (top right).

An additional means of finding the sex of a lovebird is by visual examination of the cloaca. If the tip of an auroscope (a device used to examine the ears) is inserted a little way into the vent of a bird, a rudimentary examination should reveal that the hen has a minute pair of raised 'dots,' which are the openings to her ureters (the kidney ducts), and a larger, single opening, where her oviduct opens out. The male also has the two urethral openings; however, there are also two other small protrusions where his vasa deferentia (the sperm ducts) open out. It is recommended that a small amount of local anaesthetic be dropped into the vent prior to examination. The application of the anaesthetic will paralyze the terminal bowel for a while and diminish the tendency to defecate. This practice invariably necessitates the use of two people and considerable experience. It is a most effective technique, but only with sexually mature birds.

Another process by which one can ascertain the sex of the birds is chromosomal karyotyping. The sexes differ as to the number of paired chromosomes in each body cell: the male's sex chromosomes are equally paired, while the female's are considerably mismatched in size. This procedure is highly technical, however it is standard practice in gynecology and genetic counseling. A method of differential staining which picks out the sex chromosomes of birds also exists. This test is completely reliable and holds no danger for the bird.

A surgical procedure (laparotomy) that will reveal the ovary or testes of the bird is available. Local anaesthesia however is necessary.

Finally, sex can be determined by comparison of the ratio of the sex-steroids secreted in the bird feces. Although this particular test is quite complicated and extremely technical, it has been made available to British breeders through the Zoological Society.

When purchasing lovebirds, make sure that you can always return one of the pair should you discover that you have two birds of the same sex.

Shown is a blue peach-faced, just one of the many beautiful color mutations of the peach-faced lovebird. Photo by Dr. Herbert R. Axelrod.

Nyasaland lovebirds breed almost constantly and should be allowed a break by separating them in the winter. Photo by Horst Mueller.

The green pied peach-faced is one of the more colorful mutations of the peach-faced. Photo by Dr. Herbert R. Axelrod.

This is a beautiful yellow mutation of Fischer's lovebird. There are fewer color mutations in Fischer's lovebird than in the peach-faced. Photo by Horst Mueller.

# 6. Care of Our Birds

If we are going to keep lovebirds and other dwarf parrots, we will need a good aviary, a balanced diet to offer them and a bird population that gets along well so that the breeding season will not cause us unforeseen difficulties.

Let's talk first about the feeding of the birds. Some bird breeders assume—and, of course, quite incorrectly—that a dish of seed (and probably a rather limited assortment at that) and a dish of water are sufficient to assure a healthy life for their birds. At the very least, lovebirds and other dwarf parrots should be offered the following assortment of seeds: yellow, brown and white millet, rye grass seed, white seed, maw-seed, niger seed, rape seed, and linseed (not absolutely essential), hemp and sunflower seeds (cracked as well as uncracked). The last seven seeds are often mixed together, much to the enjoyment of the birds. Experience has taught us that all the species prefer a diet that is as varied as possible, particularly during the breeding season, when they are molting, and when it is cold. At those times they really enjoy oil-containing seeds.

In the wild the birds must act as their own physicians, so that they instinctively know what is good for them. A monotonous diet is often the cause of certain deficiencies of which we are not always immediately aware. To allow our birds to help fulfill some of their own needs, we should offer them the universal food mixture of 'nightingale' food (soft foods) in addition to their normal seed supply. For extremely healthy birds, you will also give them plenty of greens, sweet fruits (on a regular basis), insects, ant eggs, small meal worms, enchytraea, etc.

Before we go into greater detail about feeding requirements, we would like to make a few more general remarks. Never give your birds seed that has spoiled; neither should it be too old. As it is, birds in the wild pick only unripe seed, while in captivity they have to settle for dried seed. From this we can conclude that the seeds we offer them should be varied.

Buy your seed only from reliable merchants; you can make a simple test that will indicate the quality of the seed. Place some seed on a saucer and add lukewarm water, replacing the water regularly. If it takes more than three or four days to germinate you should switch your seed source. Only seed that is capable of germination is rich in vitamins and is nutritious for your birds, thus the few extra dimes we may need to pay for the seed are well worth it. Good quality seed is, after all, quite necessary to the birds in order that the males be fertile and the females not suffer from exhaustion and egg-binding.

Every morning (preferably at the same time so that the birds will become used to the routine) the seed should be replaced or added to and new greens set down for the birds. The empty seed shells should be blown out of the dish before new seed is added. Fruits and greens from the previous day should also be removed from the aviary.

During the breeding season it is desirable to complete these tasks in the evening around seven o'clock. The older birds can then feed their brood in the early hours of the morning while the bird keeper is still asleep, and the fruits and greens will still be nice and crisp, since the sun will not yet have had a chance to wilt them.

**Seed**

Although mixed seed is readily available in stores, I am not an advocate of it. In the first place, the birds waste a good deal of it in an effort to pick out certain

Shown is a peach-faced lovebird in a standard show cage. Cages of this sort may be used to nurse a sick bird back to health. Photo by Dr. Herbert R. Axelrod.

The cherryhead lovebird is another color mutation of the peach-faced lovebird. Photo by Dr. Herbert R. Axelrod.

Lovebirds enjoy fruits and should always be supplied with some kind of fresh fruit. Here a lovebird is shown being coaxed back into its cage by the author using a bit of apple.

Sunflower seeds are a healthy addition to the diet of your lovebird. Remember to offer a wide variety of foods in order to keep the nutrition level of the diet high.

varieties; secondly, all birds do not need the same food at the same time, so that of the fixed percentages, one type of seed may not be touched, while there may be a shortage of another kind.

The ideal dish is one with individual compartments that would allow different kinds of seeds to be served separately. These dishes are available in pet shops, but do-it-yourselfers will have no problem in making one. In any case, do not use left-over dishes, china saucers and the like, as these are not economical for serving seed; droppings, dust, sand, dirt, bacteria, germs, etc. can also easily find their way into these dishes and give the aviary a messy and often dirty appearance.

If at all possible the feeder should be made of stainless steel or any other rust-free metal, or hardwood, such as oak or beechtree. In no way should we use materials that provide ideal hiding places for insects, mold and bacteria—in short, for all kinds of contagious agents. If we use hardwood, we should still reinforce the edges with metal strips. The front piece should be made of glass so that we can look into the automatic feeding dish and thus be warned as to when we should add more seed.

A few points to keep in mind:

1. All parts of the dish should fit snugly together so that there is no room for bacteria, etc., to grow.
2. Use only hard, seasoned wood, so that the dish will retain its original shape.
3. If the dish will be hung in the uncovered part of the aviary, cover the outside with good quality exterior paint.
4. It is advisable to add a "mess trough" under the actual "eating trough," which will save a lot of otherwise wasted seed.
5. The front of the feeding dish should be of glass, the roof slanted, going down towards the back and not in

The blue mutation of the masked lovebird is bred especially well in Southern California, where the weather is ideal. Photo by Horst Mueller.

The silver peach-faced is a lovely color mutation of the peach-faced. Photo by Dr. Herbert R. Axelrod.

Two more mutations of the peach-faced lovebird are shown here. The uppermost bird is an albino and the lowermost a golden cherry lovebird. Photo by Dr. Herbert R. Axelrod.

the direction of the "mess trough," with regard to possible soiling.
6. If possible, place the feeding dish in the covered section, and in any case always in the same spot. Lovebirds are habitual about where they look for their food. In fact, some birds that have been caught and were accustomed to looking for their food on the ground have died from starvation, even though a full feeding dish was located right above their heads. For this reason it is advisable to keep an eye on new birds to make sure that they have discovered the location of the feeding dish. If necessary, help them through the initial period by placing a small amount of seed on the ground.
7. In connection with the nature of lovebirds and other dwarf parrots, it is best not to make the dishes too large, so that they require filling at least once a week. In this way, the seed will never have a chance to become stale.

To those breeders who still prefer a mixed seed combination the following formula with proportionate amounts is suggested by E.N.T. Vane: canary seed (10); white millet (3); panicum or brown millet (2); small and/or cracked sunflower seed (1); mixed grass seed (1); hemp (½). A separate mixture of oats and buckwheat would be very much enjoyed by your birds and should be offered regularly; it can also be offered loose in the automatic feeding dish. For obvious reasons, the feeding dish should not be placed under sitting or sleeping perches.

**Greens**

The simplest way to provide greens for your birds is to plant some (wild) bird seeds in a sunny corner of the aviary where the birds will happily peck away at the sprouting plants. The seeds can also be planted under the feeding dish, where they will sprout quite nicely.

Young lettuce, dandelion leaves, Brussels sprouts, cabbage, chickweed, clover, spinach, shepherd's purse, etc. can be thrown on the ground, though it is more hygienic to place the greens in a rack in small pieces. No doubt the birds will pull the better part of the rack apart, but the greens will probably remain somewhat cleaner.

**Fruit**

All lovebirds and dwarf parrots love fruit, particularly apples; they also enjoy sweet orange sections, pieces of soft pear, peaches, soaked raisins and currants, pieces of bananas, etc. We should place a selection on a shallow dish daily, but as all these fruits spoil quickly, the supply should be checked periodically.

**Tree Twigs**

Included in the daily diet should be twigs or small branches of willow, hazel, peachtree and elderberry to enable our lusty gnawers to gnaw to their hearts' content. An additional benefit is that some of the saps have high nutritional value. When the red coloring on the birds' plumage may appear to be fading, branches with pine needles attached are recommended to restore the original coloring.

**Universal Food (soft canary food)**

Although this food is not often given to lovebirds and other dwarf parrots we can certainly offer it to our birds, and if they seem to enjoy it, have it available in the aviary. This food is generally offered in glazed ceramic or galvanized metal chicken feeders and the like. Only give moderate amounts so that it will not spoil, because even a small amount of spoiled food can cause illness. Keep this in mind particularly when there are young birds that are being reared on "universal" food. Either place the dishes in the covered section or attach a little roof to the dish so that the rain cannot get to the contents, which would hasten spoilage.

Note the beautiful colors of the green pied peach-faced lovebird at left. Below are standard peach-faced lovebirds. Photos by Dr. Herbert R. Axelrod (left) and Horst Mueller (below).

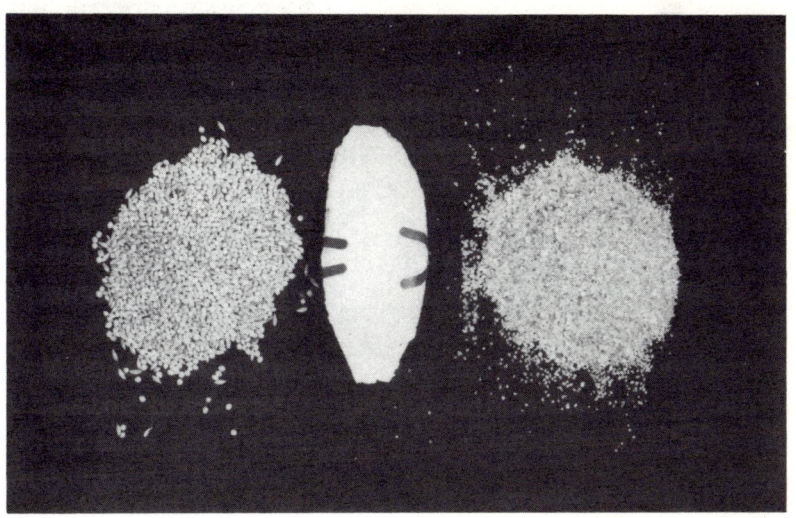

Cuttlebone, grit, and seeds treated with cod liver oil are all important elements in the diet of your lovebird.

## Cuttle-bone

Calcium is a necessary element in the diet of lovebirds, especially the younger ones, but all too often birds kept in captivity are lacking in this food source. The easiest and most economical way to ensure that your birds get enough calcium is to give them cuttle-bone, which comes from the back plate of the cuttle fish.

This plate or shell is released after the dead cuttlefish decomposes and is found on beaches, although of course, it can be bought in stores. Besides being very rich in calcium, cuttle-bone contains other minerals necessary for the good health of the birds. It should be hung up (with or without a metal holder) in any covered section of the aviary where it will remain dry. Never forget to have cuttle-bone available for your birds, particularly during the breeding or molting seasons. Another element that should not be lacking in the diet is grit.

Lovebirds can be trained to eat from a spoon, an action that may be useful in coaxing a freed bird back to its quarters or in administering medicine.

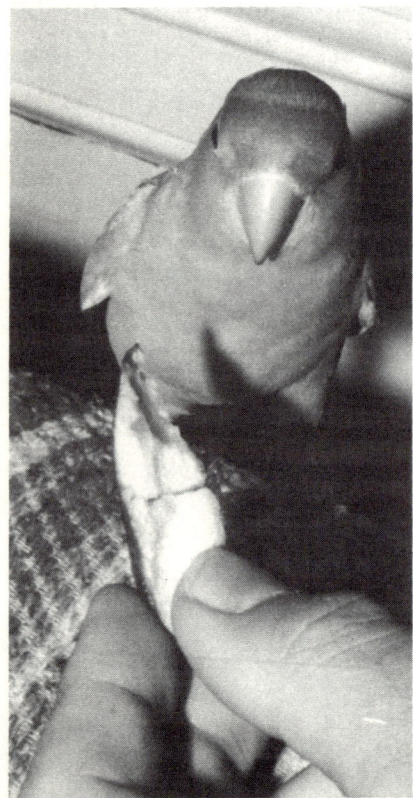

Many bird breeders overlook the importance of fruit in the diet of their lovebirds. It is essential to the nutrition of the bird, and lovebirds thoroughly enjoy small bits of soft fruit.

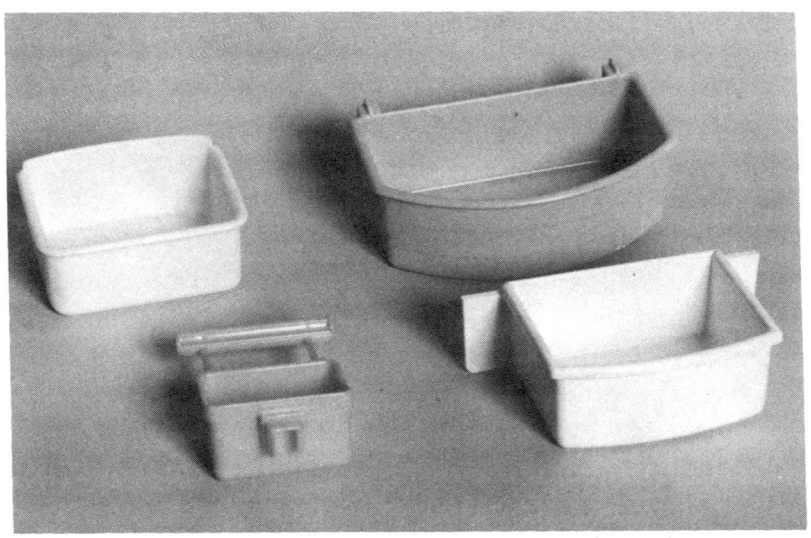

A variety of feeders is necessary to hold all the different kinds of foods you will need to offer your lovebird.

Parakeet foods are a suitable addition to the menu of your lovebird.

## Drinking and Bath Water

The best provision for drinking water is still a small rock with a drainage gutter, while a shallow basin will serve as a bathing facility. The birds will then have clean and fresh drinking water on a continual basis (although dwarf parrots do not drink very much) and an excellent bath. The only drawback is that during freezing weather the entire "water works" has to be closed off. This method provides ideal water facilities for the greater part of the year, however. Unfortunately, it is not always possible to have this kind of set up, and we must make do with automatic water hoppers, with which we would have to be content during frosty weather. Keep in mind that the drinking dishes must never be used for bathing; a wire covering will prevent this from happening. Most birds enjoy washing themselves as much as we do, so we should provide shallow earthenware dishes filled with clear water. Of course we will have to replace the water regularly; also, the dishes should be placed where they are not likely to stand in the line of fire of bird-droppings, such as under perches! To keep sand and dirt from entering the little baths, we should place them on tiles or flagstones. A sprinkler system installed in the aviary can provide an excellent bathing facility for your lovebirds. It is advisable, however, to install the control valve outside of the aviary, so that you will not unnecessarily disturb the birds. Some *Forpus* species, which will be discussed later, do not bathe but like to roll about in grass that is wet with dew or rain. If you happen to have a miniature lawn in the aviary, so much the better! I have noted earlier that it is sensible to take lovebirds and other dwarf parrots indoors for the winter, but if this is not done cover all water dishes with wire during freezing weather. Frostbite on feathers, etc. is, of course, the end of the line for your birds.

Lovebirds enjoy bathing and should always be provided with a shallow dish in which they can splash around to their heart's content.

## Perches

Of the most commonly used perches, two kinds should be obtained for our birds: those that can be attached in a stationary position and those that can be affixed in a swinging position. They should be made of hardwood. The swinging perches serve as play-ground toys and the stationary ones as resting benches. Both are indispensable during the mating season.

In aviaries that have lots of shrubbery, the various branches also serve as sitting and sleeping perches; some species, especially exotic birds, even build their nests between the branches. Particularly during the summer, the birds make much use of the bushes, yet it is still desirable to construct separate sleeping facilities in the inner aviary and in the covered section; these should be round, stationary perches placed in draft-free locations. We keep mentioning hardwood since this is most likely to remain free from lice and best withstands the insatiable gnawing of our hook-beaked friends. The perches should not be too thin, as our birds should not be able to completely encircle them with their toes but be able to completely relax on them. These perches will also help discourage overgrown nails and be an aid in developing and retaining supple leg muscles if we ensure that the perches are not all the same thickness.

Perches should be neither too rough nor too smooth, and should be replaced when they become dry and lose resiliency.

Lovebirds and other dwarf parrots instinctively like to sit high-up, so place the perches as high as possible. If the "roof" is not constructed of double wire, then do not go too close to it, as the birds might become the victims of cats and other preying animals. This is one reason why a double "roof" with about ten cm in between is highly recommended. Double-wire is also economical outside the "walls" since all parrot varieties like to clamber along the wire, and might easily become prey. Don't be cheap with the perches; your birds should not have to fight for a sitting or sleeping place! Naturally, no perches should be hung underneath another one, since the droppings of the birds on the top might fall on the birds below them. The same goes for hanging perches above any food, water or bathing dishes.

Perch covers serve a dual purpose in the cage or aviary of the lovebird. They clean and trim the nails, and they also protect the perches from the constant gnawing of the birds.

It is best to install perches along the sides and walls of the flight and shelter in order to allow sufficient space for the birds to fly about unhindered. This will also permit the keeper to move freely about in the aviary to perform necessary chores with no danger of running into one of the perches.

One should carefully observe the reactions of the birds to the perches, as well as the other equipment provided for them. If the equipment is not being properly used, changes should be made to facilitate a more beneficial use of these materials.

## The Bath

We have already mentioned water baths; however, many birds very much enjoy a sand-bath. If you do not have a nice dry spot with clean sand in the aviary, you can provide a sandbath on earthenware saucers. Although most lovebirds and other dwarf parrots seldom use the sandbath, it can still be useful to have if one is keeping different types of birds (although we do not recommend this). *Forpus* species rarely take a water bath; these birds like to roll in grass that is wet with dew or rain, as mentioned earlier; they also very seldom take a sand bath.

## Nest Material

Usually included in the description of the various species is a general discussion of the building materials that are used by our little hook-beaked pets. However, it is useful to know that the bathing dishes are not used exclusively for bathing but also for soaking all sorts of nest materials. Grass, bark and the like are first dropped into the water before they are used to make the nest. Sometimes the birds omit to take some material out of the water, in which case the bird keeper should remove it and place it next to the bathing dish. Later on the birds will choose whatever they wish to use.

Keep in mind the importance of having nest material handy for your birds, even after the nest has been completed. During the actual breeding they may want to make some adjustment to the little "nursery," and if they cannot find the necessary material, they may suddenly stop the breeding cycle. The following are some of the building supplies your birds can use: hair, grass, hay, spraymillet stems, dry grasses, dry leaves, raffia (unpainted), small pieces of bark and twigs from the willow, elm, hazel, elderberry and pear and other fruit trees.

There are some breeders who feel that damp peat is always an essential material to use as a filler for the nest box. In my own experience, I have often found this particular medium unnecessary, and sometimes even a deterrent to breeding. It has been observed that some birds find the peat quite undesirable and become so obsessed with removing it that they allow their entire breeding process to be interrupted by this action. Occasionally, eggs that have already been laid can become buried and crushed in the hen's feverish attempts to eliminate the peat. There have been reports that damp peat will avert 'dead in shell' eggs by raising the humidity of the nest box. Indeed, this material will perform this function; however, the moisture that emanates from this substance will dissipate long before the eggs hatch, and it is really only at hatching that the eggs require the additional humidity. Nevertheless, a dry atmosphere is not the only cause of 'dead in shell' eggs. Embryo mortality is the greatest during the first three or five days and the last three or four. At these times, 25 and 50% (respectively) of all embryonic deaths may occur, regardless of the moisture level of the surrounding environment. During the first few days, poor hygiene, extremes in temperature, and sudden jolts to the eggs are the most common causes of fetal extinction. But the later fatalities may result just as much from a cold, damp nest box, as from a desiccated environment.

Do not think, however, that no form of litter is needed in the nest. Some form of filler is necessary to prevent the eggs from cracking against one another and also to absorb the feces of the chicks. However, if provided with some sort of softwood to chew at, the birds themselves can outfit their accommodations with a filler that is satisfactory to them. Instead of being expelled from the nest, this filler will then be used by the birds to be shaped into a well-defined nest for the eggs.

## The Floor

It is not a simple matter to maintain living plants in the aviary; however, the effort that goes into it is well worth it. A lawn is ideal in the open as well as the closed section of the aviary, but if we plant seed, this should take place quite a while before the aviary becomes the domain of the birds. Using sod is certainly a lot simpler and faster. If one still prefers to use seed, mix in a little canary and weed seed with the grass seeds. Use a very hardy type of grass seed. If your floor is made of concrete, add a thick layer of soil. Of course the grass will have to be sprinkled often, but an added benefit to this is that many birds enjoy cavorting on wet grass.

It won't be necessary to mow the grass as the birds will keep it short. During the fall when the birds are moved to their winter home, the lawn can be mowed and fertilized (not with chemical fertilizer) or covered with a thin layer of peat moss. In the spring it will probably be necessary to add a few pieces of sod or plant some new seed in bare spots, but that should not be much of an expense. If we use seed to fill in the bare spots, we will have to protect these spots with wire in order to give the seedlings a chance to grow before allowing the birds to peck at the new grass.

## The Sick Bird

It is understandable that the lovebirds and dwarf parrots will become sick if their care and nutrition are in any way lacking. We should pay a lot of attention to giving them the best in housing, feeding and any other aspects of bird care. If we take the time and trouble to do things right, we should not be faced with all kinds of disasters. Quite often the duration of our birds' sickness is relatively short; therefore, if we are not able to catch the disease quickly, it might be too late. For this reason it is important that we familiarize ourselves with our birds by knowing their attitude towards other birds and

Your local pet shop has a wide variety of health aids available for the care of your lovebird. Ask your pet dealer or veterinarian for advice and recommendations on the use of these products.

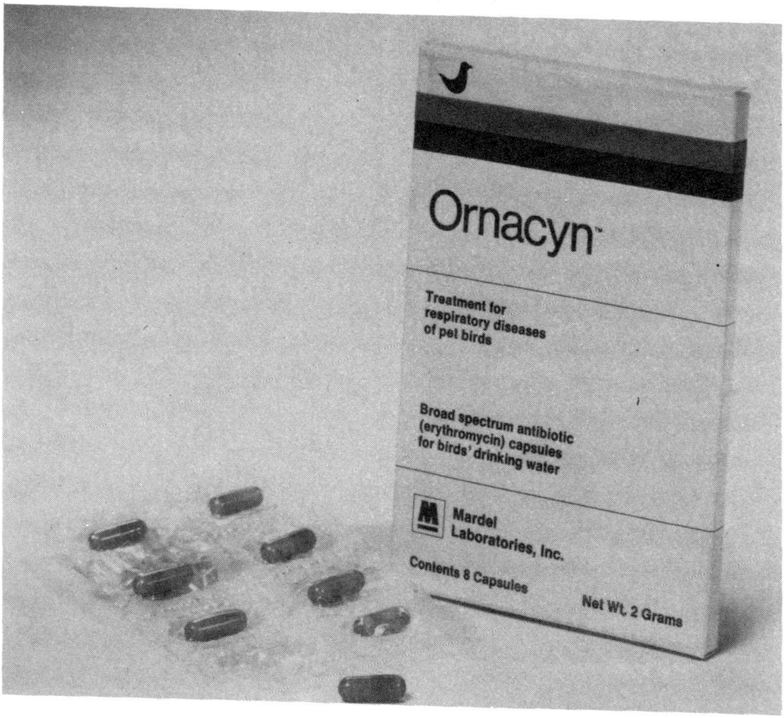

what constitutes their normal behavior.

If we observe, for example, that a bird quite suddenly is sitting in spots he normally avoids, we might take this as an indication that something is wrong. If he is making a bigger mess than usual with his food, this can be a bad sign. If he seems to be sitting in a strange way, again we should be alerted. When a healthy lovebird is resting, he generally sits on just one foot. If your bird is resting on two, then he probably is not feeling 100% healthy.

A birds' plumage should be nice and smooth, his eyes should be bright and there should not be any dirt hanging from his feet or beak. Speaking of a smooth plumage, this has caused quite a few misunderstandings. When one goes to buy a bird, one generally stands very close to the cage; after all, we want to see what we are buying. However, a bird may pass the "smooth plumage test" and still not be a healthy bird. Observe the bird you plan to buy from a moderate distance, preferably in his own 'abode' (not, if possible, in a transportation or observation cage); and you will soon know if the bird is 100% healthy or not.

Many times there are only small indications that imply that a bird is not an entirely healthy specimen. Never wait too long before taking action, as in trying to make sure that something is really wrong while waiting for more definite symptoms. It is better to be too early in taking positive action than too late; later if we should find that our diagnosis was incorrect after all we did not lose anything, other than perhaps some time. Being too careful is far better than being nonchalant. If you have doubts about a certain bird, carefully catch him —although this in itself is not too good for lovebirds, especially for the more nervous ones—and place him in a warm ($30°$-$32°$ C.) draft-free area by himself. Since these birds do not like to be confined to small areas, give him a roomy flight if at all possible, such as an attic or shed (possibly their winter home) where you can maintain a constant temperature. High temperatures make the birds thirsty and of course they will want to drink more water. This affords the ideal opportunity to add some medicine to their drinking water. This solution will dissolve in water and must contain good antibiotics that will not cause unpleasant side-or after-effects. Always ask for advice from your local pet shop or bird breeder/dealer regarding the medication.

The condition of a bird's plumage is a good indication of the health of the bird. If the feathers are not smooth, or if the bird is plucking at its own feathers, this is a sure sign that something is wrong.

Many of these preparations will stimulate the various glands that give resistance to whatever ails the bird. In addition, fertility is promoted and the shine and color of the birds' plumage are improved. In fact, it is a good idea to add a few drops of a preparation of this kind to the water of your birds every once in a while.

It is important to check the perches for all kinds of bacteria on a regular basis since parasites are often the cause of various problems. If you make these inspections every week (every two weeks during the breeding season), being careful not to upset the birds, you will avoid more serious problems. Cleanliness is an absolute must! By paying close attention, we can determine whether parasites have got in the plumage of our birds, as the feathers will have a brush-like appearance. Take action immediately! Also, if your bird(s) should show signs of losing weight, so that the chestbone sticks out, or if the bird(s) becomes overweight, as evidenced by his difficulty in moving, we must become alert immediately and separate the bird for treatment.

You can also tell if one of your dwarf parrots is ailing by checking the anal opening. This can be checked without catching the bird. If the bottom part of the bird's body is swollen, she is probably suffering from egg-binding. If the feathers around the anal opening are soiled, then we are probably dealing with diarrhea or with an intestinal problem. Of course it may be caused by a more serious disease. That's why it is important that you read a book that deals with parrot diseases.

After a bird has recovered from whatever ailed it, we should not, of course, bring it back immediately to its normal abode. The bird was, after all, in an area where the temperature had been raised as part of the medical treatment, and to bring the bird back to the aviary where the temperature is much cooler would be too much of a shock. Our recovered pet would soon be our patient again. Let the temperature in the "sick room" drop gradually until it

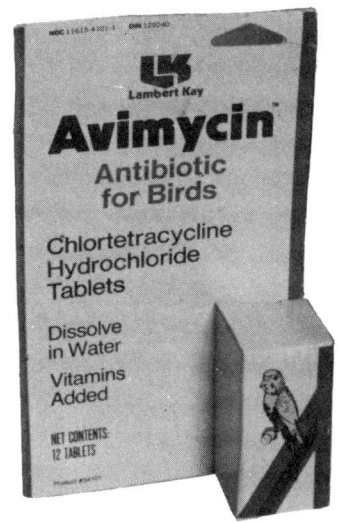

With the vast assortment of products on the market for the health of lovebirds, the serious fancier should be able to properly care for his birds with a minimum of difficulty.

reaches the normal temperature of the aviary. After that, wait still another few days before letting the bird go back outside. It goes without saying that we should choose a sunny day for this rather than one that is wet and chilly.

As stated before, it is necessary to obtain a book on parrot diseases describing the most common ailments and discomforts of lovebirds. Although we may be obligated to enlist the help of a veterinarian once in a while (especially where expensive lovebirds are concerned), we should be able to act as very good "general practitioners" with the help of *Bird Diseases* by L. Arnall and I.F. Keymer (T.F.H. Publications, Inc., Neptune, N.J.)

# 7. *Agapornis cana*

**Scientific Name:** *Agapornis cana* (Gmelin), 1788.
**Common Name(s):** Madagascar lovebird; Gray-headed lovebird.
**French Name(s):** Psittacule à tête grise; Petite perruche à Madagascar.
**German Name(s):** Grauköpfchen; Madagaskar Unzertrennlicher.
**Dutch Name(s):** Grijskop-agapornis; Grijs-maskerdwergpapegaai.

Although Rutgers *Encyclopedia* does not go into it, some authors, including James Lee Peters in his book *Check List of the Birds of the World* (1937), recognize two subspecies: *A. c. cana* (Gmelin) and *A. c. ablectanea* (Bangs). The former is found on the island of Madagascar except in the southwesterly region and the central plateau, but has been introduced into other parts of Africa and nearby areas (Rodrigue, Mauritius, Comoro Islands, Seychelles, Zanzibar and Mafia Islands). *A. c. ablectanea* is only found in the south-west region of Madagascar. The trademark of this bird is the brighter gray color of its head, neck and chest, and the sharper greens of its wings and underside.

Only ornithologists encumber themselves with these relatively small distinctions, which is a pity, since I feel the chance to breed fairly dark Madagascar lovebirds is no longer as simple as it might have been. As far as I can ascertain, both subspecies are available for sale on the market. This lovebird species is very popular among fanciers, and every year locally bred birds are offered for sale.

## COLORS

MALE: The entire head, cheeks, throat and neck and part of the shoulders and chest are whitish-gray. The birds' underparts are light grass green; the wings are dark green. The tail is green, with black feather tips. The chest has a hazy yellow glow which becomes darker toward the wings and the underside. The beak is whitish-gray, the legs are light gray and the eyes are brown. This species measures approximately 5½ inches (14 cm) in length and weighs about an ounce (30 g).

FEMALE: Because of her predominantly green colors, the female can be readily distinguished from the male. Areas that are gray in the male are a light yellow-green in the female. Her underside is also lighter in color. Generally, the tail lacks the distinct black markings of the male. The rump is light yellowish green. Beak, legs and eyes are the same as those of the male. Whereas the undersides of the wings in the male are black, those of the female are green. She measures about 5½ inches (14 cm) in length; the wings are about 3½ inches (9 cm), and the tail about 2 inches (5 cm).

OFFSPRING: The young of this species can be sexed at an early age. The young males are a more intense green on the back and wings, and the gray can be seen quite early in life, sometimes while they are still in the nest. The beaks of the females are generally lighter than those of the males.

This beautiful lovebird came into the spotlight only after the second World War. It is peculiar that the Madagascar lovebird has concentrated itself only in Madagascar, which although large, is not well situated from the point of view of expansion. Consequently, as seen from the genetic viewpoint there are quite a few variations from the other lovebird species. We won't go into that here however; the interested reader can look up my article in the *American Cage Bird Magazine*

(September 1970, pp. 27-28 "Introduction to lovebirds—VIII"). This species does not have the ring around the eye and has the smallest beak of all lovebirds.

In the wild *Agapornis cana* often travels in large flocks; sometimes these flocks can consist of 150 or more birds. They do quite a bit of damage to farmed land (such as rice paddies). The farmers, predictably, do their utmost to protect their land from these onslaughts but usually without success. The birds also feed on all types of grass seeds which they find in the fields and along the edges of forests. They live mostly along the edge of forests where there are trees that shed their leaves. *A. cana* will seldom be seen in the thick of the forest.

Madagascar lovebirds fly fast and straight. If for some reason they become alarmed, they fly up and away, disappearing in no time and screeching all the while. Because their flying ability is so well developed, it is understandable that they can travel great distances, which brings to mind the obvious question: why did this species never fly to the mainland? Their flying capabilities could easily take them to east or southeast Africa. Until now, the species has not been seen in Africa itself, except for specimens that have escaped from captivity.

The Madagascar lovebird is, by all appearances, primarily a seasonal breeder. November and December are the customary months in which breeding usually takes place. A rare handful of hens have been known to lay eggs in warmer months, but it seems to be impossible to get this species of lovebird to breed from late spring to early autumn.

The nest building habits of the Madagascar lovebird are very interesting. The birds use shallow holes in trees as well as crevices in rocks and other such places to build their nests, with tree holes being the most popular and common. *A. cana* is representative of the type of bird that makes a little "cushion" of various materials in the hollow of the nest. The female lays from four to six white eggs in this "bassinette," but in the wild we often see much larger broods; I have seen nests that contained as many as 8, 9 and 11 eggs! It is not too daring to imagine that we are dealing with a nest of two females here. However, some books and articles have noted that one female can lay up to eight eggs during one breeding cycle, although I was never able to substantiate this in the wild. The eggs measure 19-20 mm x 16-17 mm.

The female fashions her nest without the help of the male. She uses mostly leaves which she chews into the desired shape and size; the pieces are then placed between her feathers and transported to the nest. Having arrived at the building site, she stretches out her feathers, thus dropping the building materials into the nest. She may drop some on her way to the nest, and strangely enough, will rarely pick up material to put back between her feathers once it has fallen.

After the nest has been completed the breeding period begins and usually lasts about 18 days. Although it was previously believed that both the male and female sit on the eggs, more recent studies have shown this not to be the case. Only the female does the hatching; the male provides her with food on a regular basis and sometimes stays longer than necessary in the nest. Perhaps this is what was confusing in the earlier studies. In the aviary we can observe this breeding habit too, although *A. cana* is not the easiest bird to breed. However, a somewhat experienced bird breeder should be able to bring a couple to expand their family without too much trouble. If we have more than one nesting box in the aviary so that the female can make a choice, a couple in captivity should soon start to breed. Provide roomy nesting boxes so that the female can build to her heart's content. Nesting boxes that are 45 x 35 x 30 cm with an opening of 2 inches to 2½ inches would be most suitable. If you want to ensure good breeding results, place your Madagascar lovebirds in an aviary by themselves so that they need not be aggressive and quarrelsome towards other birds that share the same lodgings. (Madagascar lovebirds have been known to cause quite a ruckus with their fellow lodgers during the breeding season. The hens of this species are quite protective of their nests and, when agitated, will fluff themselves out violently. Spreading her wings slightly and splaying her tail feathers, the hen warns her intruders with a jarring screech. Any further advances upon the nest will be met by a hostile sudden shriek, which can be quite alarming to the unwelcome invader. Except for this period, they are sweet-natured and peaceful.)

For the use of nesting materials, make available all sorts of twigs, pieces of raffia, dried chickweed, leaves, coconut shell fibers, pieces of bark, dried grass and straw. Sometimes when all the eggs have been laid, the female will still look enthusiastically in the nooks and crannies of the aviary for building materials to place between the feathers of her chest, back or rump to take back to her nest. You can understand that a large nesting box will be put to good use with these species, although I have kept lovebird pairs that build nests in the nesting boxes of grass parakeets.

When the young birds have hatched after about twenty days, they are mostly covered with down, but after about one week some "feathers" have started to appear and they begin to look more like lovebirds. The parents feed their young with insects (especially small meal worms and ant eggs), as well as enchytraea, earthworms, little spiders, etc., and various seed types which certainly must not be left out of the diet. Soon after the young males leave the nest they begin to show gray markings on their heads, which is a convenient way to sex these birds.

A noteworthy thing about this lovebird species is that they do not have the prominent eye-ring on their feathers, or on the skin. And their whitish-gray beaks, as previously stated, are the smallest of all the lovebird species.

In the beginning of this chapter we noted that *Agapornis cana* is capable of doing a great deal of damage to crops. Consequently the birds were originally exported in great quantities. Sometimes there were as many as several hundred of them sitting in shipping crates! Because lovebirds are easily stimulated to fly madly about, their wings were clipped, with the result that they started to peck at each other's feathers. The unfortunate consequence of this is that most of the Madagascar lovebirds arrived almost bald.

I am sure that every reader will conclude from the above that *A. cana* is suitable for keeping only in roomy aviaries where they can fly all they like. Only when the birds are kept in a roomy aviary will they breed, although even then we should not expect everything to fall into place, so to speak. First we must devote ourselves primarily to the acclimatization of the birds; for they can still present us with problems before they have adjusted to their new lodgings and become comfortable with their environment. Becoming accustomed to living in captivity is anything but easy for lovebirds since by nature they so love freedom, wide open spaces and flying. Fortunately, these birds do not arrive as timid and in as poor a condition as they did twenty and more years ago. Even so, we must take very precaution with them.

It follows that the shrubbery should not be too dense,

as it would then interfere with the birds' straight flights. It is also my experience that the birds should be in the outside aviary only during the summer (and perhaps during the spring and fall, depending on your particular climate) if we are to prevent eventual fatalities. It is also my experience that these birds are not as strong as they are presumed to be in many books and magazines. From all of the aforementioned, we can presume that it would take a somewhat experienced bird breeder to successfully breed Madagascar lovebirds. Beginning bird breeders would be well advised to start with the lovebirds that are described in the following chapters. The Duke of Bedford let Madagascar lovebirds breed freely on his estate in England until he came to the discovery that the birds had difficulty surviving the winter and in some cases simply could not make it. Let this example be a warning that during the winter months the birds should be provided with housing that is sunlit, heated and roomy. To avoid fighting, it would be best to separate the males from the females so that the males cannot hear or see the females; this will prevent the birds from constantly flying into the wire.

Fortunately, feeding products available on the market today for the various cage and aviary birds are well balanced, having undergone numerous tests, so the result is that broods are bred without too much difficulty. Still, we know all too little about the development of the young babies from the moment they crawl out of the egg until they leave the nest. With the help of nesting boxes equipped with glass back panels, we have attempted to solve some of these mysteries, but up until now without very much new information coming to light.

During these periods of observation I did notice that the initial feeding of the young takes place quite quickly and that their heads were not initially pushed back and up to receive food but were laid to rest in the left or right hollow of the shoulder. Possibly this method is used in connection with the complicated shape of the beak. I have further noted that the female behaves quite differently in the wild as compared to the aviary, as evidenced by details I have collected. In captivity it is the female who is more inclined to continue to fight and quibble with her spouse and the other birds in the aviary. The female also seems more nervous, more impatient and quicker to fly off the handle than the male, who will soon become accustomed to his new lodgings and from then on not be likely to cause much trouble.

Due to the character and attitude of the female, eventually the male's good nature will lessen somewhat, and he may even get to the point where he will fight with his spouse and other females; it stands to reason that not much good will result of the breeding process under those circumstances. Only by separating the birds and placing them with different partners will we have a good chance for a few more years of successful breeding. Yet it should be noted that breaking up couples will not always enhance breeding activities. Some breeders opt to leave the quarrelling couples together but will put them in a new home; exchanging aviaries can help enormously. At first the birds will busily inspect everything. Of course we should take advantage of this opportunity to provide them with nesting boxes and stimulating food so that they will soon start to breed.

It can be safely stated that *A. cana* individuals are somewhat timid, and sometimes even rebellious, although they can become very sweet to their keeper and often so tame that they will peck at food in the keeper's hand! One of my males even learned to say a few words; his pronunciation was hardly proficient, but it was understandable nevertheless. Of course the taming of the Madagascar lovebird is relative and depends very much upon the manner in which they are treated. It is easier to tame the males than the females, for the latter usually respond to a friendly display of affection by creeping into a corner and acting like indignant, spoiled children who are not getting their way! If we carefully pick up a female *A. cana*, she will twist herself around by using her claws and beak in a painful manner. Be careful or you might be a victim of a nasty bite! I once had such a "bite" treated by a doctor who had to give me two stitches. Take care when handling the birds for whatever reason, and do wear gloves. It is hard to believe that such a relatively small beak can exert such strength, but believe me, the bites they are capable of giving are vicious and deep!

We have made a few remarks about breeding in the aviary. I would now like to go into a little more detail on some of these pointers. As stated before, the best thing is for these birds to have large nesting boxes available to them. We should also arrange for plenty of nest building materials to be transported to the aviary since the female uses quite a lot in building her nest. At this time the birds should be left undisturbed, for with the least provocation the female could very well desert the eggs and the nest and start on another nesting box. Even when the female has selected a box for breeding, we should not take the other boxes out of the aviary for the same reason that it would not be the first time the female suddenly left her eggs to begin on a new brood. Inspecting the nests is, of course, not advisable, which should not be surprising considering the nervous nature of these birds.

Various articles in bird journals have claimed that bird breeders obtain the best results when they do not make any plans or effort to stimulate the birds to breed. Personally I have found this to be so in quite a few instances: Just as I was thinking, "I wonder how my canas are doing?" I was surprised to find a nest with half-grown fledglings in it! It is also a good idea to leave the birds alone when you notice that the male is starting to feed the female. He fulfills his natural duties best when no one is paying attention to him, but if we still choose to observe what exactly the male plans to do, he will perform his duties rather tentatively and very carefully. Certainly this will not help the breeding process very much.

Let's go back to the breeding box from where the babies crawled out of the eggs after about 23 days. Between the first and the last babies there is quite a time span and understandably so, since the female started sitting after the first egg was laid. For forty days the young stay in the nursery, where they receive devoted care from the parents. At the time that they leave the box they can already fly quite well, and at this point the male takes charge of most of the rearing that is left to be done. However, he appears to prefer his daughters over his sons. While the male will feed his daughters with much enthusiasm, sometimes he may totally neglect his sons or drop them by a feeding dish as if to say, "There's the food—now try to help yourself!" One certainly does not come across something like this every day in the fascinating world of birds.

For the first few evenings the father will direct his offspring to the nesting box where the whole family will spend the night together. It is a fascinating sight to see Dad do his best to get his brood in bed before dark! Usually he will herd them into their original nesting box, but sometimes he will choose a different box for spending the night. This is another reason why we should let all the nesting boxes remain in the aviary.

It is wise to separate the young from their parents when they have become completely independent. If this is not done there is a good chance that not much will become of the next brood. It is also possible that the young birds may start to mate, with incest offspring the result. Not to mention egg-binding, unfertilized eggs and other problems. It is understandable that the young birds should be housed indoors during the winter in roomy quarters that separate the sexes. Incidentally, I am sure that it will be clear to everyone that birds bred locally can deal with local weather a good deal better than those that have just come directly from Madagascar. Locally bred birds also seem a lot less nervous and timid and less inclined to bite!

In conclusion we want to direct your attention to the correct feeding requirements of your birds. As we know, most lovebirds live on brown millet or panicum, spray of millet, all sorts of grass seeds (especially rye grass seed), canary seed with millet and unpotted rice. Even though the birds may not want to eat certain foods, try to accustom them to variety. Once they develop a taste for a certain food, they will enjoy it. They also need crushed hemp in limited quantities but increased somewhat during the breeding season. They cannot handle whole sunflower seeds, but will simply devour cracked ones. Lovebirds do not care for greens very much, although from a health viewpoint it is a good idea to make some available to them (also in connection with the building of the nest; see above). To help them satisfy their urge to gnaw we should hang fresh twigs or branches in the aviary once in a while, and of course we must not forget to replace daily the drinking and bath water.

Tame *A. cana* individuals, i.e., birds that have completely lost all timidity, can make outstanding show birds, but it is not a simple trick to teach them to "stand" for the judges, and that could easily lose some points. As far as I know there has been no cross-breeding with other lovebird species registered to date. The announcement of a successful product of the Madagascar lovebird and the budgerigar is yet a fairy tale, although the famous lovebird breeder Mr. M. Beetz (Geldrop, Netherlands) says, "The possibility exists if we cut the tail feathers of the parakeet (do not pull them out, however, because they will then grow back in)." This crossing was announced in 1890 in a German paper called "Gefiederte Welt."

There have been no color mutations reported with the Madagascar lovebird; however, it seems that such mutations should happen as frequently with this species as with any other lovebird. For example, imagine the enchanting appearance of a blue with a gray head. The possibilities are quite attractive.

On the subject of acquired colors, Mrs. E.A.H. Hartley (1909) reported an older hen that lost its green coloring during the autumn molt. The back developed feathers that were near black, the breast turned red, and the upper tail feathers became orange. The bird died, however, a few months later.

We would like to conclude this chapter with a general remark. In this book we speak regularly about different mutations (i.e., variations from inherited characteristics that arise suddenly and generally without cause; new color combinations and shades in color arise from these mutations). Readers who want to become involved in this very interesting hobby—which of course requires quite a knowledge of genetics—are advised that the color breeding of lovebirds parallels that of the budgerigar. It is not within the scope of this book to delve deeply into the subject. Any good book on budgerigars should send you quite a distance on your way, at least theoretically. And of course apart from following our directions as carefully as possible, you will need. . . lots of luck and patience!

# 8. *Agapornis personata fischeri*

**Scientific Name:** *Agapornis personata fischeri* Reichenow, 1887.
**Common Name:** Fischer's Lovebird.
**French Name:** Inséparable de Fischer.
**German Name(s):** Fischer's Unzertrennlicher, Pfirsch Köpfchen.
**Dutch Name:** Fischers dwergpapegaai.

*Agapornis fischeri* is currently known as *Agapornis personata fischeri*. This little parrot inhabits the region that is south and southeast of Lake Victoria and lies more northerly than the habitat of *Agapornis personata personata*. In fact, one could say that Fischer's lovebird lives in East Africa north of Tanganyika.

Since this subspecies is kept by more fanciers than any other lovebird, we want to discuss it in as much detail as possible.

**MALE AND FEMALE COLORS:** The back, chest, and wings are green; the neck is a golden yellow, while the cheeks and throat are orange. The top of the head is olive green, the forehead is a lovely tomato red. The feathers just above the tail are blue, the tail is green with sky-blue tips and with an indistinct black band shortly before the ends. The roots of the outermost feathers of the wings are brownish-red underneath. The beak is red with a white curved line that runs along the top of the beak. There is also a similar white border around the eyes, which are brown. The legs are slate blue. This subspecies measures a good 4 inches (10 cm), the wings are about 3¼ inches (8 cm) and the tail is 1 and one-fifth inches (3 cm).

OFFSPRING: These look much like their parents except that their colors are somewhat duller, and the base of the mandible has brown markings. Other details can be found on page 147 under *A. p. personata*.

This dwarf parrot was discovered by Dr. G.A. Fischer on his expedition from Pangani to Lake Victoria. Reichenow named this species after it's discoverer. The early records of Fischer's lovebird correlate almost exactly with those of the masked lovebird with the exception that Mr. K.V. Painter of Cleveland, Ohio was able to import only one such bird in 1925. In 1926 there was a tremendous European influx of this particular lovebird, and, as is characteristic with newly-imported lovebirds, they almost immediately went to nest. By that November, Herbert Whitley of Paignton Zoo had fledged young. This achievement, however, went unreported until Prestwich gave an account of the incident in his *Records*. Prior to this, the first reported breeding was credited to the Marquis of Tavistock, who fledged four offspring on January 11th, 1928. It is also quite possible that they were first bred in Germany in 1928, because by 1931 the Berlin Zoo had reared 68. In France, Decoux also bred them in 1928. Fischer's lovebird is quite readily bred, and it is reasonable to believe that in Europe they have been breeding every year since their arrival.

No doubt this subspecies is the most well known and the most popular (but not everywhere) lovebird of them all. It is ideally suited to aviary life and is a diligent breeder besides. Care and breeding requirements are not difficult; in fact, even the most inexperienced of breeders can confidently buy a pair of Fischer's lovebirds and hope for success—providing of course he does indeed fill these requirements. You will be well advised to buy your pair from a respected dealer, however, since many times one will need to be exchanged. Sexing them is not a simple matter, so that it is quite common to end up with two males or two females instead of a true pair. Make sure that the birds you buy have achieved their true color since breeding with birds that are too young is not a good idea. It will promote egg-binding and produce weak fledglings. In addition, the females may not provide enough food for their young, or possibly even desert them altogether. If we are in the possession of a really good pair, we can be assured of excellent breeding results that may prove profitable as well. Naturally this does not imply that we should abuse our birds! Only when we promote breeding each year with care and consideration, can we count on really healthy babies for which there will be a big demand.

*Agapornis p. fischeri* lives at elevations of 3,200-5,700 feet (1,000-1,750 meters) where there are considerable temperature variances and sometimes long dry spells. It prefers to live in isolated clumps of trees with grass plains between them. It also likes to fly to the *Acacia, Adansonia* (baobabs), *Commiphora* and *Balanites* trees that grow in the open plains. The breeding period starts during the last few days of, or a little after, the rainy season. The trees and shrubbery have then been rejuvenated and have absorbed the necessary moisture. The birds are quick to take advantage and gnaw happily away at twigs and young leaves, or bring them back to the nest to feed to their young. (Keep this in mind for the inhabitants of your aviary.) Besides greens they eat various grass seeds as well as acacia seeds and millet in the wild. One needs to offer a similar diet in the aviary. They take their time in satisfying their hunger, spending hours at a time in search for, and consuming food. Naturally, when they have young to tend to they must go about this business in a more efficient manner. They live in small flocks whenever and wherever they land and they must be on the look-out for bird-catchers (human), which on the whole they seem to be able to elude quite well. Their flight is straight and fast; the rustling sound of their wings can be heard along with their high-pitched chirping when in flight, and the chirping is audible at considerable distances. *A. p. fischeri* breed in colonies. According to Vane, birds of this species that have escaped—either from an aviary or from a bird market—will form their own colony, regardless of where they may find themselves. Man has attempted to start colonies of this species in the wild in various places in Europe, but they have not been able to survive for any length of time due to the number of "bird-catchers" that are always hunting them. I do not know if there are still colonies that were started by escaped specimens.

They are hunted in their native countries also due to the enormous damage they can do to crops. The farmers use all kinds of means to be rid of them, including poisonous seeds as well as guns.

It is quite remarkable that *A. p. fischeri* and *A. p. personata* do not hybridize (breed with each other) in the wild, although they will do this in the aviary. Their natural habitats practically border one another. (Man has introduced *A. p. fischeri* to a much more easterly region, namely around Tanga, where, since 1928, they can also be found in the wild.) Beautiful cross-breeding results have been achieved with birds in captivity, with, among others, *A. roseicollis*, *A. p. personata*, *A. p. lilianae*, and *A. p. nigrigenis*. It would appear that cross-breeding results have also been established with the blue *personata*, but this mutation, as with the lutino, has also not been properly fixed even though there are still occasional reports in both the United States and Europe of blue fischeris and lutino fischeris. Yellow, greenish-yellow, and white mutations are presently still being bred.

Fischer's lovebird is a popular species for cage or aviary and, when given proper care, can be an excellent breeder.

In addition to what was already written about their menu, there are a few more details that can be added: apart from the normal variety of seeds we should daily offer fresh, soft willow twigs, greens, grass and weed seeds and soaked rye bread—especially during the breeding period. This "rearing feed" can be made extra effective by adding a few drops of cod liver oil. Soaked wholemeal bread crumbs also do an excellent job of feeding the young. Both the bread and the cookies can be soaked in milk or even water with some honey or pineapple juice added; a few drops of cod liver oil here again will do much good. If the parents should desert their young for whatever reason, we can easily rear them with the help of a plastic eye dropper. Of course in that event the mixture will have to be very smooth as any lumps will clog the eye dropper. One of the advantages of rearing the young birds oneself is that they become very tame, friendly, and affectionate, which cannot always be said of birds bought as adults. If feeding requirements are not fully met, it is not unusual for parents to start "feather-picking" their young. Obviously, this does nothing to promote proper growth in the young birds. It is quite remarkable that even in the wild, should the birds be driven from their natural habitat due to forest fires, or war, etc., they would adapt themselves to their new environment and the food available to them, although often still lacking one or two necessary elements in their diet. Several nests have been found in regions where the birds had been thus affected which contained chicks that had been plucked bald. Let's hope that these birds have since returned to their original homelands, and that peace may prevail for the sake of both man and beast.

*A. p. fischeri* is being imported in large numbers, but I would still recommend locally bred fischeris to the beginner bird-fancier. This will eliminate the necessity of acclimatizing your new birds—which is not an easy task. One can then also ask for advice from the seller about his specific birds. Even though this species breeds in colonies in the wild it is a good idea to separate the pairs for breeding regardless of the size of the aviary. The best breeding results are obtained when the various pairs occupy separate but adjoining 'cages.' The pairs need not be of the same species. Not infrequently two different lovebird species may be hanging on opposite sides of the wire that separates them, and chirp sweet nothings to each other. When brought together and housed by themselves, this may very well lead to a successful cross-breeding. It is certainly amazing that birds in captivity may cross-breed relatively easily, whereas this never occurs in the wild. To the best of my knowledge, *A. p. fischeri* is the only species where incest takes place in the free state. Mothers and sons, fathers and daughters, brothers and sisters will mate together regularly. In light of this it is important, of course, to separate the young from the parents as soon as this is feasible.

One might presume from all of the preceding that keeping and breeding *A. p. fischeri* is child's play; this, however, is not the case. Only when the best of care is extended to our birds can we expect good breeding results and healthy birds. Only when we keep within the guidelines that experts have taken years to establish can we be assured of success.

One great advantage of this species is that the birds do not seem to object to nest inspections. This does not imply that we should be constantly looking inside the nesting boxes; that just might backfire on us. Before we go into more detail on breeding in the aviary, let's go back to the "wild" fischeri. As already stated, *A. p. fischeri* breed in colonies, but contrary to the statement in several books, not always in hollow trees. They also very much like to build their nests in the perfect little spaces provided by the joints of the palm leaf and stem. In addition, they might choose suitable little spaces in the breadfruit tree. In areas where escaped birds have started their own colony, their nests can even be found in buildings. Sometimes their nest is a "normal" *Agapornis* creation, while at other times it might be an oval shaped affair with an overhang. Nesting materials consist of not-so-fine pieces of vegetation which are transported by the beak, not in between the feathers. In the aviary we should provide these birds with twigs and small branches from which they will strip the bark to use as nesting material. We can also provide them with strips of paper (thick paper if possible); obviously not newspaper as the ink is poisonous.

In the wild this species lays about five or six white eggs; in the aviary this will vary from three to six. The eggs are laid on alternate days and the female starts sitting on them as soon as the first one has been laid. Should she desert the nest, try to replace her as soon as possible with a grass parakeet as surrogate mother, preferably a young bird that has not yet reared birds of her own. This may sound strange, but the explanation for it is that an experienced grass parakeet "knows" what her chicks should look like and will get quite a fright when she sees the feathers around the beaks of the young lovebirds. A young grass parakeet, on the other hand, will not be aware of this and will feed them as if they were her own. The nesting box is lined with twigs and grass, etc. The hollow of the nest will be partially covered by a kind of overhanging structure. All nesting materials are transported by the beak. It takes 3-3½ weeks for the eggs to hatch. After about 35-37 days the young will fly out of the nest; sometimes this takes even longer. About another ten days later the young are totally independent, and it is best to separate the young from the parents at that time for previously mentioned reasons. Vane mentions a case that happened in the United States of a bird breeder who had two females and one male. Both females laid eggs and had two young each from this same male who fed both his "wives" and his young in turns. Vane correctly adds that this must be a unique case, and that it is highly unlikely that this would occur again. Vane also mentions the case of a hand-fed *A. p. fischeri* that was brought up together with a grass parakeet and learned to say "sweet" and "pretty boy." I must say I'm skeptical because it is virtually impossible to teach a fischeri to talk. As I mentioned, it is possible to have two pairs breed in the same aviary since they are, after all, colony breeders. However, I would advise that we limit this to two pairs per abode for the good of the breeding results in general. If we have several broods in one aviary the females will also feed the young from other nests and when there are several couples together, this can lead to brood disasters. Some young will be overfed while others are forgotten or neglected; in addition, it is difficult to provide exactly the right kind of food for such a large group housed together.

It is probably quite well known that there are also yellow fischeris. However, this mutation was much more popular before World War II; nowadays, we only see an occasional yellow fischeri, either at exhibitions or in the aviary of a specialized fancier. Doubtless their high price has much to do with their waning popularity. Still, things seem to be picking up because various breeders in Japan and the United States are having success with their yellow fischeri broods year after year. Do not attempt to breed mutations with birds that are not old enough, however, as the offspring will not have a particularly strong constitution, nor will their colors be as attractive as they might.

## COLOR MUTATION

An important color mutation of *Agapornis personata fischeri* is the blue mutation. This mutation is somewhat smaller than the wild bird and has an extremely pale gray head. It was first bred by R. Horsham in South Africa around 1957. Two years later, in 1959, it was bred in San Francisco, California by Dr. F.B. Warford. The method for obtaining the blue mutation of *A. p. fischeri* is as follows:

*FIRST YEAR*
Blue *personata* x wild form *fischeri* (*nigrigenis* or *lilianae*). The offspring of this pairing will have the blue factor split.

*SECOND YEAR*
F1 (offspring from blue *personata* x wild *fischeri*) x wild form *fischeri* (*nigrigenis* or *liliana*). 50% of the newly-formed F2 generation will have the blue factor split.

*THIRD YEAR*
F2 x F2 (mutual). With any luck, in this pairing we will mate two F2's with the blue factor split, yielding 25% blue *fischeri*. If, however, only one of the F2's has the blue factor split, 50% of the F3's will have only the blue factor split.

In any case, bear in mind that it is wrong to mate an F1 mutation to a blue *personata*, as the F2 from such a match will be hardly discernible from the blue *personata*. For this same reason it is not recommended to pair two F1's, because the end result will again be F2's that are almost exact replicas of the blue *personata*.

## HYBRIDS

*Agapornis personata personata* x *A. p. fischeri*
*A. p. lilianae* x *A. p. fischeri*
*A. p. nigrigenis* x *A. p. fischeri*
*A. p. fischeri* x *A. p. personata*

A. p. *fischeri* x A. p. *lilianae*
A. p. *fischeri* x A. p. *nigrigenis*
A. *roseicollis* x A. p. *fischeri*
A. p. *fischeri* x A. *roseicollis*
A. *taranta* x A. p. *fischeri* (by Mr. L.A. Ara, Calcutta, in 1952—See: *Avicultural Magazine*, 1952, 36).

# 9. *Agapornis personata lilianae*

**Scientific Name:** *Agapornis personata lilianae* Shelley, 1894.

**Common Name(s):** Lilian's Lovebird; Nyasaland Lovebird.

**French Name:** Inséparable de Liliane.

**German Name:** Erdbeerköpfchen.

**Dutch Name(s):** Nyasa-dwergpapegaai; Nyasalanddwergpapegaai.

Lilian's lovebird is a subspecies of *Agapornis personata*. It lives in Nyasaland and Northern Rhodesia.

**MALE AND FEMALE COLORS:** Primarily green in color, the underside being a little lighter; the forehead and the crown are tomato red while the cheeks and throat are paler, more of an orange-red color. The green tail has a yellowish tint at the base and a dark band shortly before the tip of the tail. The tail starts off green, but later ends up with a base that turns to an orange-red. The beak is red, the feet are grayish-brown, and the eyes are brown. This species measures 4½ inches (11 cm), the wings are 2 and three-fifths to 2 and four-fifths inches (6.7-7 cm), the tail is 1 and three-fifths inches (4 cm). The female is identical to the male, although sometimes the red on her head is a little less bright. Her eyes may be a shade lighter. There is also a slight weight difference between the sexes of this species, the female weighing about 43 grams and the male about 38 grams.

**OFFSPRING:** Duller in color than their parents, with the green and red colors somewhat darker. The color of the cheeks is still a little vague.

*Agapornis personata lilianae* was first discovered in 1864 near the River Shire in Nyasaland. At the time,

The Nyasaland lovebird is a true colony breeder; there have been results achieved with multiple broods in the aviary.

however, many did not realize this to be a separate species but thought it to be *Agapornis roseicollis*. Thirty years later Shelley fully described *Agapornis lilianae* in the bird magazine *Ibis*. He named the species after Lilian Sclater, sister of the famous ornithologist P.L. Sclater (author of *Systema Avium Aethiopicarum*, among others). Bird fanciers did not respond with much interest and it was not until 1926 that the first specimens arrived in England. In that year, Captain Stokes gained a medal from the Avicultural Society when he fledgled the first offspring from this newly imported species. Also in 1926, Mme. Lecallier of France bred the Nyasa, but had far better results than did Captain Stokes. On March 28th, she put her fourteen birds into an outside aviary, and by the end of May she had twenty fledged chicks. By the end of the year, she had reared an additional twenty chicks. In 1928, Tavistock stated that the chief aim of the Nyasa lovebird was to perpetuate its own kind, and it would breed almost constantly, with only a slight break for molting. At about this same time, Mr. F. H. Rudkin, a most experienced breeder, called this species the most prolific of all the lovebirds. At first these birds were recognized as *A. roseicollis* until they were acknowledged to be *A. lilianae* by the English breeder D. Seth-Smith.

There is very little to say about their life in the wild; it is best to refer to the other subspecies that have a white eye-ring. They do prefer to live in close proximity to water, such as near large rivers. Nevertheless, they may be found in various elevations ranging from 1,600-4,900 feet (500 to 1,500 meters) above sea level. Their habitat practically borders that of *A. p. nigrigenis* yet the two species do not cross-breed with each other, even though there may be only a strip of 50 miles (80 kilometers) between their homes. Most of the imported birds come from Rhodesia and Nyasaland, although the lutino variety hails from Australia. This mutation is a bright yellow and has a red head. Outside the breeding period, *A. p. lilianae* wander about in groups of 30-40 birds. One can hear their shrill cries as they fly overhead searching for water or food. Their menu consists of the various kinds of seeds, berries, and fruit, though their preference definitely goes to unripened millet. The local farmers see them going rather than coming, and they are capable of doing considerable damage to crops. When the breeding period has almost arrived, the birds break up into smaller groups and go looking for suitable nesting places. Not much is known about their breeding habits although it is claimed that they like to use old weaver nests, but they also like to use all kinds of tree holes and the like.

Although these birds are real colony breeders, and results have been achieved with multiple broods in the aviary, we still advise you to separate the various couples and house them in adjoining brooding cages or small aviaries. They bring nesting materials to the nest by means of their beak, not in between their feathers. Once the nest has been completed, and quite often this includes a sort of overhang, the female will lay between three and five white eggs which she will hatch in about three weeks. The male will feed her and also helps in rearing the chicks once they have flown out of the nest at about 30-35 days. Especially during the breeding season it is important to offer plenty of greens, even though the birds do not take much of a fancy to them. If there is a shortage of vitamin D, the female may start to pluck the feathers of her young. A number of companies manufacture excellent vitamins (sold in pet shops), that can be mixed in with the seed. Their problem can be treated by mixing about three drops of cod liver oil with two pounds of seed, and giving plenty of cuttle-fish bone. Some *A. p. lilianae* like to eat soft fruits, but unfortunately this is not true of all of them. We also want to add germinated seeds, spraymillet, and soaked white or rye bread to their menu, and we must not forget the oft-mentioned willow twigs. Once the birds have been brought to breeding condition, we must keep a strict eye on matters as they will continue to breed throughout the year if we do not take the necessary precautions; it is certainly not a good idea to let them breed as they will. Only spring and fall breeding should be allowed. During the winter we can separate the males from the females, but since this may cause numerous problems we could allow the more inseparable among them to stay together, but then of course we must remove the nesting boxes. If we take the birds indoors during the coldest part of the year and provide them with peaceful little places where they can sleep (not in nesting boxes) everything should work out well. *A. p. lilianae* is a very popular aviary bird, but the Marquis of Tavistock was mistaken when he thought that the lilianae's popularity would exceed that of the grass parakeet.

As stated above, *A. p. lilianae* does contain a lutino variety. This bird has a red head and collar, and is yellow on the back of the head, back, wings, tail and underside. Its beak is light red to pink. They are still quite expensive, and not readily available. In the Louise Hall inside the Wassenaar Zoo there is a beautiful pair. The first picture of this bird can be seen in the magazine *Foreign Birds* of 1956. My wife, who lived in Australia for several years before I met her, told me that she has seen one of the first lutino mutations in Adelaide (South Australia). This was in the beginning of 1960. The first specimens, however, were bred in 1933 by Mr. Prendergast, with two normal birds. When I was in Australia I had the opportunity to see hundreds of them. Seeing these birds in Australia is commonplace, although they are still expensive. They are bred regularly in California and Europe but the species as a whole is relatively uncommon in number, compared to the rest of the lovebirds. It is sensible to breed lutinos in separate aviaries because the possibility exists that the young from a regular lilianae will kill the yellow young.

Cross-breeding results have been achieved with the following breeds: *A. roseicollis, A. personata fischeri, A. personata personata,* and *A. personata nigrigenis.*

## COLOR MUTATIONS

A color mutation of the *Agapornis personata lilianae* is the lutino. The physical characteristics of this mutation are a red head and a yellow body. They are also very small in size.

The first recorded breeding of this particular mutation was in 1933 by Prendergast in Adelaide, Australia. It is quite possible that the mutation was unconsciously imported from the wild in the "split" form.

The first six lutino *A. p. lilianae* to arrive in England were exported from Australia in 1937.

It is evident that split-lutinos were in the U.S.A. many years before their presence was discovered, because in 1940 lutinos were bred in California by Mrs. Reed, and in 1951, the Rudkins, also in California, bred another.

## HYBRIDS

Hybrids occur between all the lovebirds with the periophthalmic ring (the ring around the eye).

# 10. *Agapornis personata nigrigenis*

**Scientific Name:** *Agapornis personata nigrigenis* W.L. Sclater, 1906.
**Common Name:** Black-Cheeked Lovebird.
**French Name:** Inséparable aux joues noires.
**German Name:** Russköpfchen.
**Dutch Name(s):** Zwartwang-agapornis; Zwartgezicht-dwergpapegaai.

This is another subspecies of *A. personata*. The natural habitat of this bird is a rather small region in the northern portion of Southern Rhodesia, around the Zambezi River and the Victoria Waterfalls where I had the opportunity to observe them in small groups.

Although this bird is readily enough available on the market, in its natural environment it is being threatened by extinction if the authorities there do not make stricter laws to protect this beautiful bird.

**MALE COLORS:** As mentioned, *A. p. nigrigenis* looks a lot like *A. p. lilianae*, but the forehead and cheeks are black, hence the name. Their brown eyes are encircled by a wide white ring. The feet are gray, the beak is red, being somewhat paler at its base. The rest of its body is primarily green, the underside being a little lighter. There is a vague pink blotch on the chest.

**FEMALE COLORS:** The female is virtually indentical to the male although her colors tend to be a little duller. However, since there are often such variations between individual birds, one cannot rely on this slight difference. The pelvic test is the best method for sexing this species.

**OFFSPRING:** They look very much like the parents although in their early life their colors are considerably duller. Some fledglings have black spots on the beak.

These birds, which are regularly offered for sale in pet stores and by bird breeders, do present a problem when it comes to determining their sex. The pinkish blotch on the chest does not even help us out since the female has this marking also. Perhaps the color of the

The exportation of the black-cheeked lovebird has been forbidden in order to protect its existence. There are many locally bred birds of this species, however, so it is fairly readily available to bird fanciers.

eyes can help out to some degree, since the iris of the female is generally somewhat lighter than that of the male. It is a shame that their homeland has stopped exporting them, which means we must now rely upon locally bred birds. This would not be so bad, but in Europe, for instance, this species has not been entirely pure-bred and there is quite a lot of incest on the market. In spite of the fact that it is practically impossible to obtain pure blood (it would be wonderful to be sent some "fresh blood" from Africa to help us build up our waning bird population and purify this species lineage to a degree), I still want to tell you a few things about this bird. *Agapornis personata nigrigenis* was discovered in 1904 by Dr. Kirkman, who fully described it as a full species in the *Bulletin of the British Ornithologists Club* (1906). Four years after its discovery, in 1908, the first specimens were imported into Europe. *Nigrigenis* was long thought to be a subspecies of *A. lilianae*, but more intensive studies have shown it to be a subspecies of *A. personata*.

Experience has shown that this bird is an excellent breeder in captivity. It is a sweet and peaceful bird, even when housed with fellow species or other exotic birds. They particularly like oats and unripened cherries. The young birds are fed "ant eggs," chickweed, and boiled, finely chopped eggs. The female usually lays four to six, although sometimes anywhere between two and eight, eggs that measure 22 to 23 mm. x 15.5 to 16 mm. Both male and female sit on the eggs and after about 16 to 21 days they hatch. There may be a considerable time span between the hatching of the chicks. The male does not feed the female while she is sitting on the eggs although we have observed that the female sometimes does feed the male when he is on the eggs. The young are first fed only by the male and later by the female as well; after about thirty days the young fly out.

The birds may breed some five times per year; it should go without saying that they should be limited to three times at the most in order to protect the female from egg-binding and other such problems that might arise from too much breeding.

It is understandable that the government of their home country has forbidden any catching and exporting of this species, especially when we consider that their habitat is relatively small, being around 80 miles (130 kilometers) in diameter. Catching and exporting these birds in large numbers would certainly make extinction in the wild a realistic possibility in spite of the fact that there were such a large number of them. In 1929, for example, some 16,000 of these birds were caught in one month because of the damage that they did to crops. During World War II their future looked very bleak indeed, but timely regulations enforced by the appropriate government agencies fortunately saved their pretty little necks just in time! Importation is presently out of the question, without considering any black marketing. Japan, too, has neglected to give much attention to this species in their enormous bird breeding industry, although presently thousands of bred specimens, which incidentally are very healthy and properly colored, are leaving the "Land of the Rising Sun."

The Marquis of Tavistock let several pairs live freely on his estate to see how well they could adapt to local weather, food, vegetation, etc. Everything went fine until the fall when they suddenly disappeared. Many thought that these birds had simply answered a migration instinct and returned to their homeland. But why should these birds even have a migration instinct when their original domain is just a small part of Rhodesia? It seems more likely that they became the victims of birds of prey when the protective foliage had fallen off the trees, or that they left looking for warmer climes

The black-cheeked lovebird breeds well in captivity and is a pleasant addition to cage or aviary.

although there have never been any reports to that effect.

The first black-cheeks to be imported into Europe came into Germany in 1908, followed by a much larger influx the year after. Frau J. Prove reported breeding and the young of that particular pairing fledged on September 26th, 1908. Mathias, in *Bird Notes*, discussed the astonishing vigor and productiveness of his pairs. In

1909, he fledged fifteen young from only two pairs. He also discovered that young birds began laying when only four months old. Despite this amazing breeding ability, these birds were nearly lost to British aviculture by 1925. They were imported again in 1926, and prospered until the late fifties when, once again, their numbers diminished almost to the point of extinction.

In the wild this species lives in all except evergreen forests. When I observed them for a period of more than ten days in the wild, I came to the conclusion that they are cheerful and fast, not particularly timid and that a few specimens that had been caught could be tamed in just a few days; their behavior reminds one of the grass parakeet. Of course there are differences between various individual birds, but generally they are affectionate little creatures that can be very sweet, much like A. p. lilianae. They very much like the sun and fresh air and I feel the best breeding results in captivity are obtained in outside aviaries where the nesting boxes are frequently hosed off to keep the eggs from drying out; some kind of bathing facility should be available to them so that they can take a bath regularly, preferably every day. In the wild I have observed them taking baths early in the morning and late in the afternoon in little streams and small waterfalls. Neunzig states that a pair of A. p. nigrigenis adopted and reared two-day-old grass parakeets. (Gefiederte Welt, 1911, page 230). Whether something like this has reoccurred I could not say, but it would be interesting to find out!

## HYBRIDS
A. p. nigrigenis x A. p. personata is very popular.
A. p. nigrigenis x A. p. lilianae also exists.

# 11. *Agapornis personata personata*

**Scientific Name:** *Agapornis personata personata* Reichenow 1887.
**Common Name(s):** Masked Lovebird, Yellow-Collared Lovebird.
**French Name(s):** Inséparable masquée; Inséparable à tête noire.
**German Name(s):** Masken-Unzertrennlicher; Schwarzköpfchen; Personata Unzertrennlicher.
**Dutch Name(s):** Zwartmasker-dwergpapegaai; Gemaskerde dwergpapegaai.

The natural habitat of *Agapornis personata personata* is in northeast Tanganyika, southeast of Lake Tanganyika. In comparison with most other lovebird species, the domain of the masked lovebird is relatively small.

**MALE AND FEMALE COLORS:** Blackish-brown head with yellow collar. Throat and chest are yellow with an orange-red glow. The balance of the bird is primarily green with the exception of the rump, which is bluish, and the tail, which shows a black and red band shortly before the ends on the outer feathers. The brown eyes are encircled with a wide white band; the legs are gray. This subspecies measures 5 and four-fifths to 6 and one-fifth inches (15-15.7 cm), the wings are 4 and one-fifths inches (10-10½ cm), and tail 2 to 2 and one-fifth inches (5-5½ cm). The females weigh about 56 grams, and the males only slightly less—approximately 50 grams. Male and female are absolutely identical so that it is desirable to arrange for an exchange possibility with the bird breeder at the time of purchase, should the "pair" prove to be of the same sex.

OFFSPRING: The young birds look like their parents although their coloring is somewhat duller and the black in the plumage is not very sharp. It is advisable to band the young birds early in life so that they may later be distinguished from their parents. It is also advisable to use different colored bands as soon as the sexes have been determined.

The masked lovebird is a rather aggressive bird and should be kept in a roomy aviary.

The distribution of the masked lovebird ranges from the southern part of the volcanic Meru-Essimingor ridge down the eastern side of the rift valley, and across the central railway to the latitude of Mbeya. It is bordered on the east by the Pangani Valley and further south by a group of forested mountains. In the northern half of its range the masked lovebird comes within fifty kilometers of the Fischer's lovebird, but the two subspecies never meet. The masked lovebird has no unique feeding or breeding requirements. It survives on the seeds of available trees and roosts in the crevices and crannies of baobabs. It has also been stated that this bird will nest in Indian swifts' nests and breed in the 3 inch (7 cm) space between the tiles of a roof and the boarding underneath. Often they will also nest under iron roofs, which must retain much of the high temperatures radiated by the hot African sun. In any case, the masked lovebird is quite nomadic in their quest for food, and will never willingly perch unprotected.

*Agapornis personata personata* was first described by the German ornithologist Reichenow. The first living specimens were taken out of their homeland in 1925 by an American bird fancier who was travelling through Africa. In the spring of 1926, Mr. K.V. Painter of Cleveland, Ohio became the first to breed these birds. In 1927, they became available to bird importers in great numbers. In that same year, three members of the Avicultural Society reported breeding success, the first being the Marquis of Tavistock. Mr. M.T. Allen was unfortunate enough to have his first complete nest of offspring die just before fledgling. In Germany and Switzerland, they were first bred in 1928, and in France it appears that the first breeding took place in 1930 at Cleres, by Jean Delacour. By that time in North America, the birds were nearly domesticated, and were even being bred in cages 1 x 2 x 1 feet (29 x 56 x 29 cm).

These birds are quite aggressive and need a roomy aviary. It is amazing that the masked lovebirds seem to retain their argumentative natures even when they have been in captivity for a long time, in which case this tendency may mellow a little at best!

Recently imported specimens (or those that come from Japan) require careful acclimatization. Once we have succeeded with that we should have no further problems. I would advise beginner bird breeders, however, to buy locally bred birds. There is one drawback in keeping this subspecies: the females have a tendency to suffer from egg-binding if the care and feeding of the birds is not 100% correct or if they are kept outside in an aviary all year round which does not offer a properly protected night shelter. That is why we would recommend taking the birds inside during the winter, even though they are seasoned to the cold weather.

There is now also a blue variety in this subspecies: this bird has dropped the yellow colors so that the green, blue, and yellow colors have ended up white.* At exhibitions in particular these birds draw a great deal of attention. They are reasonably good breeders although I feel they are a little less strong than the "natural" type. It is best to bring them inside during the winter, into a slightly heated space such as an attic, and move them back outside in the spring when the weather no longer presents us with cold and wet nights. It may happen that the young of the blue personata leave the nest too early, before they are fully grown. In most cases this is the aviary keeper's fault by forgetting to provide sufficient grass seeds, or perhaps he has forgotten to provide them altogether; personatas are real seed eaters! A bunch of ripe grassheads, as well as plenty of greens,

---

*Blue and yellow *A. p. personata* are genetically identical to sky blue and light yellow parakeets. Color breeding in lovebirds parallels that of grass parakeets.

young twigs and buds (from the elderberry, willow, pear, cherry trees, etc.) should be available to the birds at all times. Most of the blue lovebirds are bred in California since the weather there is so ideal. The first blue variety was imported into England from Tanganyika in 1927 and five years later already several were

Newly imported masked lovebirds need careful acclimatization in order to survive. Once this is done, however, there should be no further problems.

being bred in France. In addition to blue, there are also gray, white, and yellow mutations in this subspecies. I feel that the yellow mutation is the least successful since this bird is not a true yellow, nor is it green, but rather somewhere in between. The gray variety is more like a washed-out blue; nor is the white variety truly white. Some of the birds have little spots on their plumage. In other words, some further experimentation could be put to good use in perfecting these color mutations. With the exception of the blue color, the other colors are most strictly inspected by the experts, and Vane says: "It is to be hoped that these mutations have simply arisen as a result of breeding with normal birds and not through cross breeding with other species. Presently there is still little known about their genetic appearance nor evolution and so they are still open to further studies."

The yellow personatas unfortunately do not have much in common with the gorgeous lutino *lilianae* with the orange spots. To successfully breed blue mutations one needs: 1) a lot of sun, 2) a very roomy aviary, and 3) plenty of nesting boxes. The last two of course can be realized, but the first will depend very much on your local climate. Should your climate be less than ideal, you could use a Vita-Lite lamp (Fair Lawn, N.J.) not to be confused with an aritificial sunlight-lamp which must never be used since they will damage the eyesight of your birds; this could become a rather expensive proposition.

*A. p. personata* can be easily cross-bred with other lovebirds, which is one of the reasons why it is so difficult to buy pure-bred personatas. It is important to make sure that the specimens you intend to buy parallel the coloring as noted in the descriptions. Perhaps you could get an expert to accompany you when you go to make your purchase. In any event, do not buy birds which are not sufficiently or clearly colored, or where the markings are not entirely correct.

Willow and elderberry tree twigs are important if you wish to keep your masked lovebirds in good condition. During the breeding time it is also important to provide fresh twigs, since the bark will be used as nesting material. They transport the nesting material by means of their beak, not in between the feathers. In the wild this species builds its nest in holes in trees, nooks and crannies in buildings and walls, etc. These available spaces are partitioned off with thorn-bearing twigs, etc. so that the nest is really protected rather well. (In 1928 some personatas were moved to Dar es Salaam on Africa's east coast. They seem to have adjusted well enough and their nests have been found in that of the swift's.) Nests have also been found in the carved holes made by barbets (*Lybius* species). In the wild a brood generally consists of seven to eight white eggs; in the aviary, however, four to five eggs is as much as one can hope for. It takes about three weeks for the eggs to hatch. The young are covered with an orange-red down when they come out of the eggs. They fly out at about five weeks of age but will still be fed by their parents for another two weeks or more.

To begin the courting process, the dominant hen must somehow convey her willingness to breed to the passive male. She does this by assuming a fluffed appearance. The male then repeatedly bobs his head up and down while he enthusiastically sidles along a perch towards the hen. At this point, even though the hen may plead to be fed, the male will not yet feed her. This particular action takes place only after a suitable period of time, during which there is much head-scratching and twittering on the part of the male. After she has been fed, the hen will then solicit the male for copulation. To do this, she silently crouches in a horizontal position with the wings pulled slightly away from her body. Her tail is raised somewhat, her feathers fluffed, and her head is pulled up and back. The male will then mount the hen by stepping directly onto her back. Pairing usually takes several minutes, with only uninterrupted pairings being fertile. These particular behavioral characteristics are usually best seen only in birds that were complete strangers to each other prior to the courting period.

In order to achieve good breeding results it is important to maintain a certain humidity level in the aviary; it is best to start with the breeding either in the fall or the spring. Nesting boxes should be large, measuring at least 20 inches (50 cm) x 10 inches (25 cm). The construction of the nest itself is an action exclusive to the hen. If the nest chamber is spacious and there is much material to work with, the hen will build a rather large, domed nest. In limited space, the nest is not always domed. The nest hole is usually guarded by the male even though he would be no match for an adult hen. Nest protection is not really substantial, and it has been observed that other birds will perch right on top of a nest box without causing any animosity. The actual structure of the nest is woven, and the nest can be taken out of the nest chamber as a unit if the nest chamber is large enough to permit the building of a substantial nest. Otherwise, in smaller boxes, the nest may fall apart upon removal. More nesting material will be added to the nest once the chicks hatch, and it has been noted that hens will provide additional nest material if light spills into the nest chamber or if there are any sharp projections in the interior of the nest. In addition, the sanitary needs of the nest determine whether or not more materials will be brought into the nest, thereby keeping the nest clean. There should be two levels inside the box and this is important for good results. While one brood is still being fed there is always the chance that the female may start laying a new batch of eggs on the unused level. The parent birds also often use the still available nesting boxes as a place to sleep. Whenever there are baby birds in the aviary it is a good idea to give them some soaked old rye bread, with a few drops of cod liver oil added, along with the foods described in the chapters dealing with the other *A. personata* subspecies. Should something go wrong with the rearing of the brood one can always substitute a surrogate mother in the form of a young grass parakeet. Or one can also feed the young birds oneself with the help of an eyedropper, as described in the chapter on *Agapornis taranta*. Here are some details with regard to the breeding method I use: My aviary measures 26 feet (8 meters) long and is divided into compartments which are each 3.5 feet (one meter) long. These compartments are divided by double wire so that the birds can see, but cannot touch, each other. Previously we used a single sheet of wire but had an unfortunate experience that made us switch to double wire: one of our grass parakeets was gaily clambering up the wire when one of our lovebirds suddenly grabbed one of his toes with his beak. If I had not happened to be there and immediately taken care of this situation, we would certainly have had an accident on our hands. (The breeder S.J. Houtenbos appears to have had a similar experience.)

In the early spring we hang up at least three bi-level type nesting boxes in the open part of the aviary for one pair of personatas. I have kept three pairs together in one aviary a few times and provided them with ten nesting boxes to avoid quarreling. . . and was rewarded with success. If it is a warm and sunny spring we should hose off the nesting boxes each morning and night, but take care that none of the water actually seeps inside. Once in a while the birds take advantage of this artificial shower, and get under the stream of water and have themselves a great time! As a matter of fact, the masked lovebird is said to be an eager bather, and if one bird starts to bathe, the entire flock will usually follow. It has been reported that they will drench themselves in falling rain by positioning their bodies so that the underside is exposed to the rain, saturating that portion of the body. Also, they will quite often wet their plumage by rubbing up against wet foliage.

We have pointed out in various parts of this book that birds can be banded to help in identifying the sexes, and that this is essential if we plan on having our birds take part in any shows. Lovebirds, however, have their own opinion of this banding procedure and will do all in their power to be rid of them, with some very unfortunate consequences such as wounded and possibly lame legs. (According to Beetz, placing bands on both feet helps: a tight one and a loose one; the latter is removed as soon as the bird is used to it.) As previously mentioned, it is compulsory for any bird appearing in an exhibition to be banded. Personally, I am not in favor of bands, but on the other hand it is very convenient to be able to differentiate between the sexes. However, the chapter dealing with this subject should give you all the information you need to help you make your own decision about banding.

## COLOR MUTATIONS

The blue mutation of *Agapornis personata personata* is not particularly attractive; the collar, chest, and belly are a sort of off-white, while the head is black. The bill is a horn color, having also been affected.

In late 1927, Chapman received a blue male, which was then sold to the Zoological Society of London. At first it was shown as a cage bird but later was placed in an aviary to breed. By late 1929 ten birds split for blue had been produced. The blue male was then mated with one of his own split-blue daughters, who unfortunately died of egg-binding after another split-blue was produced. By December of 1930 the splits were paired, and they raised one blue and three greens.

By the end of World War II, very few blues were left in Europe, but there was hope for the blue mutation. Although no one knew it at the time, Chapman in 1927, had also imported some split-blue lovebirds (*personata*) to France. There, in 1935, Mr. M. Morin bred several blues, the descendants of which were still available at the end of 1945.

In the U.S.A. there appears to have been a few split-blues in with the original importations. In 1932 Mr. Cross, in California, was apparently the first to raise blues. In 1935 the well-known fancier F.H. Rudkin raised four blues from three pairs. When four male blues were paired to the "wild" or "normal" *personata* one of the hens appeared to be split-blue, thus making it possible to produce another generation of blues. By 1945 the blues in California were flourishing. In my opinion it is more than likely that many of the American blues are far from pure, and many have some *fischeri* in their 'blood.'

Wild (green) x Blue = 100% Green/blue.
Green/blue x Green/blue = 25% Green, 25% Blue and 50% Green/blue.
Green x Green/blue = 50% Green, 50% Green/blue.
Green/blue x Blue = 50% Green/blue, 50% Blue.
Blue x Blue = 100% Blue.

The *parYellow* mutation (recessive) is usually called yellow. Yellow appears to have retained in a very dilute form the blues and melanins of the original.

The first parYellow were apparently bred by Mr. Scheu of Upland, California in 1935. Many of the present parYellows came from his stock. Another parYellow was raised in Japan.

*Acquired yellow* is not a hereditary trait. In or around 1932 at the San Diego Zoo there was a normal *A. p. personata* which turned for the most part yellow, but nothing more was heard in regards to this mutation.

Other colors can be obtained by combining the primary color mutations; *parWhite*, for example, is produced by combining blue and parYellow. The parYellow mutation does not completely reduce melanin production, so the parWhite still has black in his mask, while the body is a very pale shade of blue. This mutation was apparently produced in Japan about a year after the end of World War II. The first Japanese exportation to Europe was most likely in 1955 (Mr. H. van Dijk, Animali-Zoo, Eindhoven, Holland presented the father of the author with three birds!).

A white *personata* was bred in Denmark from a Blue/parYellow mated to a Green/parYellow/Blue. The white bird had no trace whatsoever of a mask.

**HYBRIDS**

Hybrids occur between all the lovebirds with the periophthalmic ring and also in *A. p. personata* x *A. roseicollis* crosses.

# 12. *Agapornis pullaria*

**Scientific Name:** *Agapornis pullaria* (Linnaeus), 1758.
**Common Name(s):** Red-faced lovebird, Red-headed lovebird.
**French Name:** Inséparable à tête rouge.
**German Name:** Orangeköpfchen.
**Dutch Name:** Rood maskerdwergpapegaai.

Although not all authors agree, most divide this species into two subspecies, namely *A. p. pullaria* (Linnaeus) and *A. p. ugandae* Neumann; the latter inhabits only the eastern region and differs slightly in coloration (deeper blue rump). *A. p. pullaria* is a native of West Africa and the Gold Coast, while *A. p. ugandae* inhabits Uganda and Ruanda.

## COLORS

MALE: Predominantly green, darker on top than underneath where often a yellowish glow can be seen. The forehead, cheeks and throat are tomato-red and the beak is scarlet. The narrow ring around the eye is white, yellow or bluish in color. The rump is sky blue, but the covering feathers just above the tail are green. The primary flight feathers have black tips; the curve of the wing is black with blue. The center tail feathers are green while the rest of the tail feathers are red with a black band a little before the tips, but the tips themselves are green. The legs are greenish-gray and the covering feathers under the wings are black. This species is about 5½ inches in length and weighs approximately 38 g., making it one of the smallest mainland African lovebirds.

FEMALE: The face is orange rather than tomato-red, and this colored area is usually smaller than the male's. The covering feathers under the wings are green.

OFFSPRING: They resemble the female, although the covering feathers under the wings quickly become black in the young male.

Red-faced lovebirds are not very popular in their native land, which is hardly strange; when a flock of these birds (which consists of close to one hundred) lands on a field of millet or corn, they generally leave it in a ravaged state. They also like to eat various grass seeds and leaf buds, which does not do the forests much good. (It is not yet certain whether they like these buds for the insects that hide in them, or for the young leaves themselves.) Figs are eaten with great relish wherever they grow.

This *Agapornis* species is the most difficult to breed in captivity. This is due, undoubtedly, to their strange nesting habits in the wild. This species carves its nest in the large, still inhabited tree nest of termites, or in termite hills. According to Coelho (1977), the average size of such a nest is approximately 30-60 cm. high. They have comparatively hard exterior walls encasing an interior of several tunnels with much more permeable walls. The substance of which this structure is made consists primarily of termite feces bonded with saliva, which becomes quite firm after it dries. Lovebirds of this species have also been known to make nests in uninhabited termite "castles." This "home-sharing," a sort of boarding arrangement, can also be observed among the *Aratinga* species which live in the Netherlands Antilles.

The biggest part of the digging of the nest is the female's job; once in a while the male joins in, but this is probably to stimulate the spouse. *A. pullaria's* "lodgings" should be imagined as a little tunnel with a widened, fairly round cavity which we will call a kettle or

Shown here is a male Abyssinian lovebird. These are easy birds to keep in that they become very close to their owners. Photo by Dr. Matthew M. Vriends.

room. The opinions regarding the finishing of this room are varied. Eggs have been found that were laid right on the cellulose shavings without even a trace of nesting material, while others have been found on layers of plant-type materials. In an aviary, it has been noted that a female gnawed only green leaves from the shrubbery, placed them between her feathers and flew into her nest with them; it was not noted that she picked up dried leaves from the aviary floor. It has also been noted that the female will use small pieces of willow twigs if they are made available.

There have been reports that *A. pullaria* has bred in a regular nesting box used by other lovebirds; we find this somewhat doubtful and at best, exceptional. According to Rutgers' *Encyclopedia*, the best results are obtained by using corkboards and securely affixing these in a tree trunk; the same dimensions should be followed as those for a regular nesting box. Recently man has tried to imitate building the termite nests by filling a 44 gallon drum with peat moss. To the best of our knowledge, Mr. A.A. Prestwich was the first to announce this (1956). The peat moss was wetted before it was put in the drum, and then left to dry. The drum was opened at one end and placed in the direction of the flight. Branches and twigs were arranged on top and around it to give it a "natural" appearance. Before long the birds started "digging"; it is noteworthy that no nesting material was used, and that the eggs and later the young laid on top of the hard mulch.

Normally this species lays between four and seven eggs, which measure 20 mm. x 16 mm. The female does the hatching by herself, while the male provides her with food. Once in a while she will leave the nest to look for food herself, or just to stretch her wings. (We should make sure we do not start breeding these birds until they are completely acclimatized). It takes approximately

3½ weeks for the eggs to hatch. Once the babies have come out of the egg, they are covered with white down. They will fly out when they are about six or seven weeks old. As stated earlier, in the beginning they look much like their mother, but soon the males will develop the black feathers underneath the wings.

The division of the food among the clutch is a lovely sight to behold: the young hold their fat little heads backwards and busily flap their tiny wings; indeed, it is a sight that will fascinate the bird fancier for hours. We want to repeat here, though, that *A. pullaria* is a difficult bird to breed and is certainly not suitable for a beginning bird breeder, but is for the more advanced breeder. Keeping them should be satisfying as they have sweet and cozy natures and are certainly not inclined to be argumentative.

To the best of our knowledge, *A. pullaria* was imported to Europe in 1730 or 1731. We assume this based on the fact that E. Albin described them in *A Natural History of Birds*, which appeared between 1731 and 1738. (Linnaeus later took over this description in his famous *Systema Naturae.*) Vane says in his book *Guide to Lovebirds and Parrotlets* that *Agapornis pullaria* was pictured in a sixteenth century painting of a "lady and bird," but we cannot judge the validity of this information. In the first place we have not seen this piece of art; secondly, it is quite possible that it is not even *A. pullaria* that is pictured. It is possible, however, that Emperor Rudolf II, son of Maximillian II, kept dwarf parrots and other varietes of birds during his reign (1576-1612).

As we mentioned before, all specimens imported at that time arrived in a deplorable condition. For example, their wings had been clipped much too short, with the result that many of them died a few weeks later. Presently large quantities are being imported in much

A peach-faced lovebird peeks out warily from a shelter of foliage. Photo by Dr. Herbert R. Axelrod.

**Opposite:**
Closeup of a peach-faced lovebird, showing the subtle coloring of the head and throat. Peach-faced lovebirds are aggressive during breeding and should be kept in pairs in a separate aviary. Photo by Dr. Herbert R. Axelrod.

better condition and are being offered for sale in most pet shops.

Recently imported birds should be acclimatized with the greatest care if they are to survive in a different climate. Warmth, rest, a good size aviary and a balanced diet are the first requirements. Getting them accustomed to the aviary and the food may take quite a sacrifice on our part since the birds are extremely timid and nervous and will start flying about wildly with the least provocation; that is, if their wings have not been clipped. Due to their nervous natures, *A. pullaria*

Wing clipping is necessary in some cases to protect a nervous bird from harming itself by flying wildly about the enclosure.

generally undergoes this 'operation' shortly before being transported; this has both its good and bad aspects. The birds cannot injure themselves as readily in the aviary since they will not be able to fly at dangerous speeds, but they may also become more nervous than they already are, having had to submit to the wing-clipping procedure. It would seem to me that the best method is to place the birds in a roomy aviary that they have to themselves in a peaceful location; the location should be indoors even if they arrive in the middle of summer, unless you live in a climate that is reasonably close to that of Africa. In the beginning you should try to curb your curiosity and avoid seeing your birds as much as possible. Keep them indoors until the following summer. When they are ready to be moved, have the outside aviary completed with the food and water already served, and only then take them outside. Leave the birds at peace again, and after a week or so you can sit with them and quietly observe them. Their difficulty in getting used to a different climate is quite understandable as is their nervous state; they have been the target of all kinds of weapons because of the destruction they wield on the fields of the native homelands.

We strongly urge you to handle your birds as little as possible; sometimes for reasons unknown a bird can go into shock from which it rarely completely recovers. A.A. Prestwich has related that, even when taking all possible precautions, he himself had lost quite a number of these timid birds. Any unexpected or sudden movement could prove fatal for one of these faint-hearted creatures.

Moving them from the indoor to the outdoor aviary remains a risky business. However, it still needs to be done, and if we work quickly and carefully it should not be too bad. After all, the birds will have to be moved again to their winter lodgings when that time comes...

Shown at the left and below are silver peach-faced lovebirds. The silver mutation is a rather beautiful and unique variation of the peach-faced. Photos by Dr. Herbert R. Axelrod.

The albino and golden cherry lovebirds shown on this page are beautiful mutations of the peach-faced. When cross-breeding for color mutations such as these, the fancier should take great precautions to preserve the pure race. Photo by Dr. Herbert R. Axelrod.

these are chances we have to take, since there is no choice in the matter.

You should make white millet available to them, for often they will want to eat just that. This would be much too limited a diet, as you can understand, so they will have to become accustomed to other foods as well. You could mix the millet with white seed. In addition, they will need brown millet, maw seed, panicum, etc. They will keep coming back to the millet, but we must continue to try to get them used to the other seeds, as well as soaked seeds (offer only in limited quantities) and stale bread soaked in milk. You can give them sweet fruit, greens and honey spread on a slice of rye bread. Grit, cuttle-bone and fresh water should be available at all times, and it would not hurt to add a few vitamins (drops) to the bread soaked in milk. The latter is particularly useful during the time that there are young birds that have to be fed; small pieces of liver and kidneys (dried), ant eggs and a mixture of egg-yolks and chopped meat are also highly nutritious during this period. Don't forget mealworms; the birds can eat these in large quantities.

It has been said that this species makes dull pets. I don't agree at all. Once the birds have become accustomed to their new surroundings, they climb around the cage or aviary by making use of both beak and claws. The cage should definitely be made of metal, since *A. pullaria*, particularly when confined to a small area, will soon gnaw at anything that even resembles wood.

The song of the male is quite pleasant and is composed of various tones, none of which could be called loud or irritating.

Once in a while two males or two females may act as if they were a pair (i.e., male and female)—at least as far as that is possible—but sooner or later they will break this relationship and form a pair with more suitable partners.

*A. pullaria* in captivity prefers to sleep in the open air, not in a nesting box or the like. Frequently they can be seen hanging by one claw with the head facing down in the manner of hanging parrots and parakeets. We do not consider these birds very suitable for shows, with the exception of those that have been born and bred in captivity. (The road to obtaining such specimens, however, is long and difficult.) If we do feel we have birds that have completely adjusted to their aviary life and have a great affection and friendship for their keeper, we could take them to an exposition, but would have to be very wary for any disturbances to the birds.

## COLOR MUTATION

At this time there are scattered reports of color mutations of *Agapornis pullaria* being produced in Switzerland, but the mechanics of such an undertaking have not been divulged.

The amount of pied in a bird, such as the green pied peach-faced above, is determined solely by chance. Photo by Dr. Herbert R. Axelrod.

**Opposite:**
The normal green peach-faced has less color than the green pied mutation but is still a very attractive bird. Photo by Paul Kwast.

# 13. *Agapornis roseicollis*

**Scientific Name:** *Agapornis roseicollis* (Vieillot), 1817.
**Common Name(s):** Peach-faced lovebird; Rose-faced lovebird.
**French Name(s):** Perruche à tête rose; Inséparable à face rose.
**German Name(s):** Rosenköpfchen; Rosenpapagei
**Dutch Name(s):** Perzikkop-dwergpapegaai; Rozeborstdwergpapegaai.

There are two subspecies of *Agapornis roseicollis*. The first subspecies, *A. r. roseicollis*, which was probably already discovered and documented by about 1817; the second subspecies, *A. r. catumbella* (Hall), discovered in 1955 and recognized by its brighter colors.

The beautiful colors of *A. r. catumbella* (Hall) are noteworthy and certainly worth mentioning. The rose color of the head is considerably brighter, and the throat has a hint of lavender on it. The green colors are deeper, especially on the back, wings and flanks. The rump is deep purple rather than blue, and the iris is a deep brown. The beak is rosy-white with green dots. This bird is an inhabitant of Benguela, a region in Angola. As far as I know this subspecies is not available on the market; neither have I ever seen them in the zoos of Australia, Europe, Japan and United States. I did have the pleasure of seeing them in bird parks in Africa, and was really impressed with their beautiful full colors. Vane mentions in his book that Mrs. Hall, who both discovered them and gave them their name, brought a few stuffed specimens to England to show at the British Ornithologists Club in 1955. But let us now confine ourselves to the "common" *Agapornis roseicollis roseicollis*, which is kept by a great many fanciers.

## COLORS

MALE: The forehead, cheeks, chin, throat, and area just above the chest are a soft pinkish red, the forehead being the darkest. Most of the rest of *A. r. roseicollis* is bright green in color, the underside being lighter with a hint of yellow. The rump and covering feathers above the tail are bright light blue, while on the green tail there are some black and rust colored feathers. The eyes are brown, the beak is yellow to very light green and the feet are greenish-gray in color. There is a very vague ring around the eyes. This species measures 6½ to 7 inches (16-18 cm), the wings 4-4½ inches (10-11 cm) and the tail 1¾-2¼ inches (4½-5½ cm). It is the largest of the lovebirds.

FEMALE: The green and blue colors and particularly the orange in the tail are considerably less sharp than the male's colors, although the beak is darker in color. In spite of these small differences, it is still quite difficult to determine the sexes.

OFFSPRING: The young birds are grayish-green in the beginning and lack the red coloring on the forehead; the color of the cheeks is paler than in the parents.

According to Vane, Angola and southwards to the banks of the Orange River is the range of *Agapornis roseicollis*.

The peach-faced lovebird is certainly a species that ornithologists like to work with, as evidenced by the number of times this species has been moved around in the ornithologically determined "family tree" of the birds. Many experts have been somewhat at a loss with this species, and not too long ago (in 1946) the renowned Boetticher suggested that the peach-faced lovebird belonged to the genus *Amoradis*. Nevertheless, *Agapornis roseicollis* retained its name and position in the family tree, so we will leave it at that for now.

The Abyssinian lovebird is believed to have first been imported to Europe in 1906. Photo by Dr. Matthew M. Vriends.

Of all the color mutations of the masked lovebird, the blue mutation, at right, is the most succesful. Below, the mutations of the peach-faced lovebird are far more numerous and varied than the mutations of the masked. Photos by Dr. Herbert R. Axelrod.

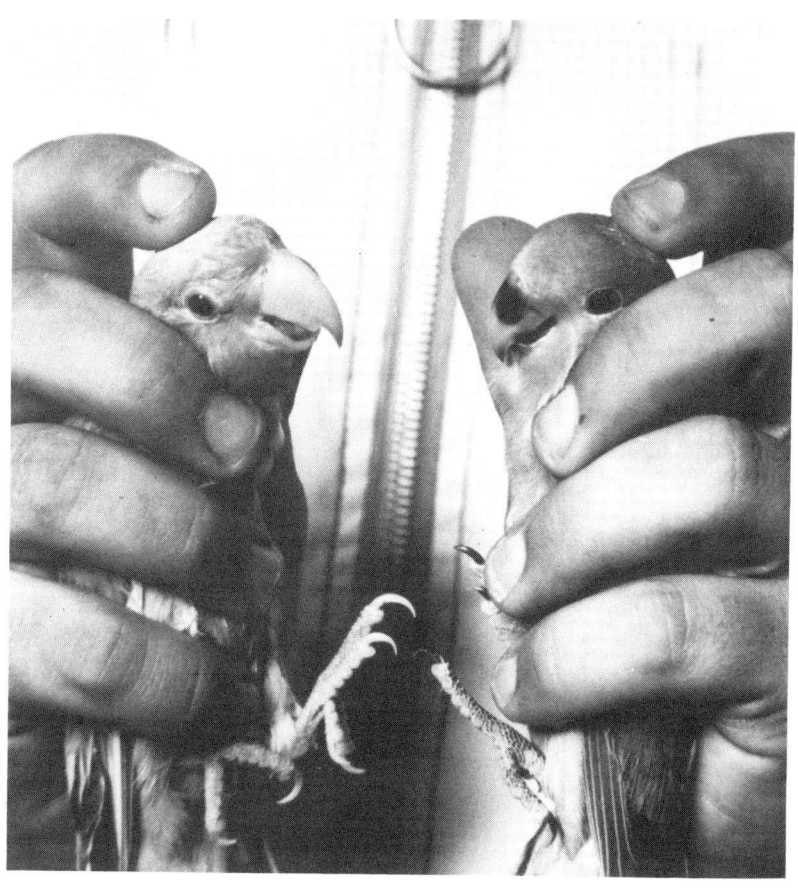

In this picture a young peach-faced lovebird is compared with one that has reached maturity. The young bird still has the dark patch on the beak, and there is no rose color on the head.

In the wild *A. roseicollis* species live in comparatively small groups, mostly in areas that are dry and grow leaf-shedding trees, though they are usually in the vicinity of a body of water. These groups of birds consist of about ten to fifteen individuals, which is in contrast to most other species that live together in far larger flocks. Often they can be seen in areas that are 1,500-2,000 meters above sea level, and they are indeed very capable of handling all sorts of temperature changes. Peach-faced lovebirds are expert fliers; their flight is straight and fast, and somewhat resembles that of the partridge, with regular intervals of gliding. During this gliding or sailing through the air, the birds can be heard calling quite loudly, more so than in normal flight. The sound is sharp and raucous, and when a flock is on the ground or in the shrubbery looking for seeds, berries or other fruit, they often let out a deafening screech, something they also like to do in a cage or aviary once in a while.

The nesting habits of these birds have been described countless times by various authors. In my book *Papegaaien en Parkieten (Parrots and Parakeets)*, I mentioned that in the wild most of the nests are found in old nests of weaver species, such as *Pyromelana nigroventris*, *Pyromelana franziscana* and *Plocepasser mahali*. I suggested the possibility of both bird varieties, i.e. the weavers and the lovebirds, living together amicably in one nest. As I see it, Vane drew a correct conclusion when he said that lovebird nests can also be found in the nests of other birds that were not weavers at all but were similar to them, either in the design of the nests, their habits or their plumage.

Several ornithologists are of the opinion that a peach-faced lovebird does build its own nests, but next to that of a weaver species (as I have seen many times in the wild) or another bird. Still others believe that the peach-faced lovebird will take over a weaver nest and send the weaver on its way. However, I must add to this opinion that these lovebirds also move into deserted weaver nests and others that are similarly built. It is a fact that peach-faced lovebirds build nests themselves, many of which have been found in the crevices of rocks, grottos, dark little corners and cracks in buildings, on bridges (as our little sparrows sometimes do), in old water wells that are partially dry, sometimes close to the ground in

The female Madagascar lovebird lacks the gray head that is found on the male. Photo by Dr. Matthew M. Vriends.

The male Madagascar lovebird is brighter than the female because of its gray head. Because of this major difference in appearance, sexing the Madagascar lovebird is no problem. Photo by Dr. Matthew M. Vriends.

ruins, but seldom if ever in trees and bushes.

*A. roseicollis* is supposedly the first species to have been seen transporting nest-building materials between its back and rump feathers. The design of the feathers is marvelous; each feather has a brush-like tip that turns or can be turned inwards and is ideal for holding nest materials in place. The feathers, of course, fit together beautifully, but considering that there are parrot types that have similar feather designs and never transport anything between the feathers, it must be assumed that the primary purpose of this particular feather design is to retain body warmth, and secondly to facilitate the transportation of nest-building materials.

Fortunately we know more about the breeding habits of *A. roseicollis*. The female lays four to five eggs (27-27.8 mm x 17-17.4 mm), laying one egg every other day. After laying the second egg, the female alone starts to sit on the eggs while the male faithfully and regularly comes to the nest to feed her. Their behavior is similar when they are kept in aviaries, and it is my hope and belief that eventually aviary keepers will solve all the nesting mysteries that remain.

The young birds are at first covered with orange-red down that changes to gray quite quickly; after about ten days the fledglings have a grayish tinge to them. After 30-38 days the young first fly out of the nest but will continue to be fed (mostly by the father) for some time to come, while the mother starts laying new eggs or looks for a new nesting box. It is she who will transport the materials to the nest sometimes accompanied by the male, who does not know the art of transporting materials between the feathers; his role is to help build the nest in the chosen box.

In spite of their raucous song, these birds are very popular pets partly due to the fact that they are excellent breeders and can breed and rear three clutches

The peach-faced lovebird is kept by a great many fanciers and is a colorful bird.

At left is a modification of the peach-faced lovebird. Note the peach-colored spots on the body; these spots are missing in the wild birds.

Above and opposite, below are black-cheeked lovebirds. These birds are excellent breeders in captivity. After 6 months the sexes can be distinguished by the pelvic bone test. Photos by Horst Mueller (left) and Dr. Matthew M. Vriends (top).

per year without problems. It is commonly believed that the peach-faced lovebird is a seasonal breeder in the wild. In captivity, however, it has been found that they will tend to breed year round. This fact seems to lead to the conclusion that these birds are not seasonal breeders by nature, but merely opportunists, breeding whenever and wherever conditions are suitable. According to the "British Museum Catalogue" this species was discovered in 1793, but was thought to be *Agapornis pullaria!* It was not until 1817 that *A. roseicollis* was recognized as a separate species. Around 1860 Hagenbeck imported the birds into Europe. They became popular immediately, in spite of the fact that they can be quite troublesome both with their fellow species and with different birds, even large parakeet types. Needless to say, it is advisable to keep peach-faced lovebirds in aviaries separate from other lovebird species, which, of course most bird fanciers do.

The peach-faced lovebird was one of the most popular species among fanciers following World War II, due not only to their smooth colorful plumage, but also because of their ambitious breeding habits; in fact, they even offer good possibilities for cross-breeding, strange as that may seem! Besides possessing a quarrelsome nature, however, their raucous tone can be irritating at times and particularly indoors; these are two points a bird fancier should keep in mind.

One must be quite cautious in making living arrangements for these birds. We will illustrate with a couple of examples which will show that this species can fool even the most experienced of fanciers. A certain pair of peach-faced lovebirds were peacefully perched and very well behaved at the pet shop, hardly making a sound; they just sat there and quietly murmured to each other. When I brought them into my home they started up such a racket that I thought I would lose my mind! I have known a group of eight birds—four pairs—that were living peacefully together for quite some time. At a certain point in time they had to be moved to considerably smaller quarters. I carefully caught them and took them all together to their new abode, which they promptly started to inspect. They continued their peaceful existence for at least another five weeks. However, when someone cut the grass in front of their aviary with a self-propelled lawn mower one day, it became too much for one of the males, who became hysterical. He started up a terrible screaming, attacked the other males (one of which became seriously injured) and generally had the whole aviary population in a terrified state. I had to separate the pairs immediately in order to avoid more accidents.

From other fanciers I have learned that not only the males but even the females fight under such circumstances. It is not rare for some of the birds to become seriously injured and perhaps even die. It would be a good idea, therefore, to house each couple separately. Experience has also taught me that it is wise to separate the young birds from their parents as soon as they become independent. After a while, even the parents can be a threat to the young birds; some bird breeders have shown me dead birds that upon closer inspection proved to be dead young birds which had not yet been separated from the older birds. It should be obvious that this species can cause considerable problems.

After they have been ringed, if this indeed is our intention, the independent young birds can be kept together for the first two or three months. As soon as they show signs of wanting to mate we shall need to become alert since at this point they can easily be the cause of fighting in the aviary. For the most part the young start to prepare for breeding much too soon. If we want to avoid weak offspring, insufficient broods, egg-binding,

It is easy to see why the peach-faced lovebird pictured here and on the opposite page is one of the most popular species of lovebirds on the market today. Their beautiful colors attract many fanciers. Photos by Dr. Herbert R. Axelrod.

etc., then we should wait until our young lovebirds are at least one year of age; generally they are not successful breeders until that time. Even the first brood of those birds that have reached the suggested breeding age is not as good as it would have been later.

The best results are obtained in an aviary rather than a cage, even if it is a roomy cage, although sometimes there are exceptions. This is understandable in light of the peach-faced lovebird's active nature; it would naturally require more living space, since this is one of the largest of the lovebird species. They are very content with an aviary that measures 2 m long x 1½ m deep x 2¼ m high. In such an aviary we will be able to grow some plants and place the nesting boxes along one of the walls made of concrete, not wire. In this way, the birds will still be adequately protected.

Since the housing and feeding of the birds are generally very good these days, we rarely have problems with "feather picking" any more, which was par for the course in days gone by when even the parents used to "pluck" their young. If we should come across this problem nowadays, it indicates that there is either a lack of a particular vitamin or that something is wrong in the design of the aviary that has caused the birds to become bored. In such a case the menu will have to be drastically improved, while their boredom can be diverted by hanging up ropes which will allow the birds to clamber up and down to their hearts' content. It may also help to give them a piece of fresh raw meat daily. Watch out for spoiling however, and remember that this will attract cats.

The correct diet for these birds, when kept in a roomy aviary, consists of the following: millet, canary seed, buckwheat, hemp, linseed, cracked sunflower seeds, fresh twigs (from willow, beech, hazel, elderberry, pine, pear, apple and common privet trees, for example) and fruit. Unfortunately, not many of these species like fruit, which is a shame as I have noticed that those that do eat fruit tend to have more shiny and healthy looking plumage. Offering them a variety of fruits may lure more of your pets to try it. Suitable fruits would be small pieces of apple or pear, pineapple, sliced figs, soaked currants or raisins and various berries. Don't forget sunflower seeds and hemp, which have already been mentioned. The hemp should be offered only in small quantities; one teaspoon per day (i.e., about 100 grains per pair) is more than sufficient. Once the young have left the nest, this can be increased to two teaspoons per day. Incidentally, an excellent food for the baby birds is eggs with rusks. Don't give too many oil-containing seeds, since this will promote feather-picking. These oil-containing seeds, when offered in too great a quantity, can also cause obesity in our birds with some unfortunate consequences such as partial or complete paralysis, or even stroke. If we thought it best not to offer any hemp in lieu of the above, this would not be a good decision either as a small amount is good for them. Offer all kinds of greens, such as lettuce, endive, chickweed, etc., but don't expect them to attack the greens with fervor or you will be disappointed. They do, however, prefer the greens to fruit.

Once we have come up with a good balanced diet, and the birds are eating a variety of foodstuffs, we should be rewarded with good breeding results. In 1976 one of my pairs (in Gainesville, Florida) bred and reared some 16 offspring: the first brood consisted of six birds, the second brought five into the world, and the third produced five again; in the fall this same pair had two more broods, this time three and five respectively. Naturally I arranged for this pair to have absolute rest during the winter that followed, and we planned to hold off on letting them breed again until later in the

A normal peach-faced lovebird is a beautiful addition to any aviary. One must take care to prevent any fights during the breeding period, though, because the peach-faced is quite aggressive at that time. Photos by Dr. Matthew M. Vriends.

year, rather than early spring. At the time of this writing—spring 1978—this pair is sitting on a nest containing seven eggs. Hopefully they will again deliver such good results!

The nest building habits of the *A. roseicollis* were first studied and documented by persons who held some specimens in captivity. Probably Mr. R. Phillips conducted the first such study when he wrote in 1896:

"The female flies on to a young bough of a growing tree, bites off—by passing her beak along sideways, nipping away as she goes—a strip of bark some three or four inches long, doubles it, by giving it a nip one-third of its length from one end until the two sides form an acute angle, and tucks the piece, at the angle, under one or more of the feathers of the lower back or upper tail coverts, leaving both ends sticking out.

"This performance is repeated until some half-dozen pieces have been hooked on, though the number varies according to the time occupied in obtaining the bark; she then flies off in anxious haste to the nest. . . . When on the nest the female employs her time in passing the strips of bark backwards and forwards between her mandibles, mumbling away at them until they are beautifully soft and nice." (From Vane's *Guide to Lovebirds and Parrotlets.*)

We have already mentioned that this lovebird breeds more easily in an aviary than in a roomy cage. It seems that this species shows much less interest in the nesting boxes when kept in a cage rather than in an aviary; they also have less interest in each other, which certainly is not conducive to successful breeding. In the cage the female does not transport nesting materials exclusively between her feathers, but often with her beak, which she will seldom do in an aviary where she uses her beak for climbing. It is quite remarkable that she loses very little of her cargo as she squeezes herself through the opening of the nesting box, even when this opening is somewhat smaller than it should be. Dropped building materials are rarely picked up again, and certainly not immediately. Possibly she changes her mind about these fallen pieces later, but initially whatever falls is left on the ground. In the wild I have never witnessed a female picking up a fallen piece.

There has been no report of any unique form of courtship among these birds. According to Mr. Jim Hayward, hens will frequently solicit the males to feed them by bobbing the head up and down slightly and calling, much like the Abyssinian lovebird. The hen, tilting her head and ruffling the feathers of the throat, carpus, and cheeks, then accepts the male for copulation. Both the male and female are strong breeders in captivity. This species does not have the definite eye-ring, and also is distinguished from other species by its habit of gnawing nesting material to make it softer and more pliable. The peach-faced lovebird also differs from the other species in that it does not over-furnish its nest.

The "cradle" can be described as a cup of uniform construction with the inner lining of the same material and consistency as the outer. *A. roseicollis* tends to chew its nesting material more finely than the other species. It is advisable to have more building supplies on hand for your birds, even once the nest has been completed, as they sometimes like to make a few alterations. The nesting box arrangement, hung in the uncovered part of the aviary, should be located in such a place where it will regularly receive the full impact of a shower. During a dry spell we should hose off the boxes on a daily basis, preferably in the morning hours. The birds themselves do quite a good job in keeping the boxes wet, as long as we always provide them with bathing water; besides thoroughly enjoying themselves, they also get thoroughly wet, and can then be seen entering the

The peach-faced tends to be rather aggressive during the breeding period.

nesting boxes in that condition. During the breeding period the male stays in close proximity to his partner, and flies into the box at regular intervals to provide her with food. Even so, the female does fly out of the nest once in a while, probably to stretch her wings. We have even noted that the male will pick up droppings of his spouse and deposit them far away from their nesting box. In the event that the female should die after their babies have hatched, the male will take care of them. In the aviary, however, this is not too difficult for him, since the "table is always set," but in the wild this is a different story; it takes numerous food searching trips to still the hunger of the fledglings!

As stated earlier, the male and female look very much alike. We should make arrangements at the time of purchase that would allow us to exchange one of them should they prove not to be a pair after all. Experienced breeders have no difficulty in determining the sexes; in the male the pelvic bones are touching, while in the female there is a space of up to 5 mm between them. If we have two females together they will build large nests and lay several eggs; if we have two males together, they will not build a nest (unlike Bengalese finches, for example, who will do this) except perhaps a half-hearted attempt at one, but the proper interest will definitely be lacking, so that it will not be difficult to determine whether or not we own a "true" pair. Incidentally, any exchanges should be made promptly so that there will still be time for breeding at the best time.

The Duke of Bedford kept countless peach-faced lovebirds in complete freedom. From his observations he found that they did not stray, but had difficulty in adjusting to the local shrubbery, climate and such, although he had better results with them than other lovebird species. I have personally never conducted such experiments. It would seem that certain areas in the United States have climatic conditions that, at least for some portion of the year, fairly well approximate those found in the birds' homelands. The possibility therefore exists that released birds in such areas could establish themselves in the wild. At the same time, of course, it must be realized that climatic conditions are not the only factors that determine whether a non-native species can become established; diseases, food supplies, the presence or absence of potential predators, etc., all enter the picture.

Although *A. roseicollis*, then, can be hardened for the winter season, it seems better to take them indoors during the colder months, or at least to give them draft-free and dry night quarters. Extra heating would not be absolutely essential, but we could provide them with some nesting boxes (sleeping boxes) providing the sexes have been separated to avoid winter breeding. The females must have the opportunity to recuperate during the winter time. We have hand-fed several baby birds, which soon became our close friends and even learned to say a few words. In hand-feeding birds, lukewarm water with "Breakfast Squares" (General Mills) and finely chopped lettuce works very well for rearing the youngsters and is easy to fix as well.

Vane reports that several color mutations have been made known since 1941. Mr. Sidney Porter received a dead lutino which had maintained the pinkish-red color. A few lutinos have been bred in Australia, Japan, and the United States. There have also been cases of abnormal pink birds; one of these birds, according to Vane, had pink coloring on the head, cardinal red on his body, brilliant blue on the rump, and brown wings.

Although we have discussed cross-breeding possibilities in another chapter, we want to pass on an interesting case that was communicated to me by Mr. Horten, a fancier from Pijnacker (Netherlands). He wrote, "It is a pleasure to advise you that I have successfully bred a female *nigrigenis* (from a 1961 brood) with a male *roseicollis* (1961 brood). On April 26 this pair had three eggs and on May 19 they had three babies, one of which died. On June 29, the fledglings flew out for the first time and are now (July 15, 1963) starting to show different colors. The female is presently sitting on a new brood of five eggs."

Mr. Beetz from Geldrop (Netherlands) has offspring from a female *A. roseicollis* and a male *A. p. nigrigenis*. In the September 1967 issue of *Onze Vogels* we read the following: "In the July issue we published a report from Gefiederter Freund stating that bird breeder Weber discovered a blue *A. roseicollis* in the nest of a seven year old pair. Mr. Habels from Roosendaal reported that he managed to breed blue *A. roseicollis* four years ago, is still breeding them now, and so has genetically fixed this color characteristic. He wrote that the gray heads do not remain gray but turn to a soft pink after the first molting. Breeders are currently trying to breed white *A. roseicollis* (see also *Onze Vogels* July 1967 issue, pages 532 and 541).

## COLOR MUTATIONS

In 1921 it was reported by Seth-Smith that the London Zoo had received a peach-faced lovebird that had the rosy tint of the cheeks spread over nearly the entire body. This deviation is not uncommon, but it does seem to be a non-inherited metabolic disorder, because a bird with this rosy plumage was paired with one of its own offspring and another like it was never produced.

There are a number of primary color mutations of *A. roseicollis*, the first of which is the lutino.

*Lutino* is a recessive, sex-linked trait that produces beautiful birds. The red and peach tones are retained, while the rest of the body is made a more intense yellow.

The first peach-faced lutinos were exported from North America to Europe around 1973. It is not known when it first occurred in the U.S.A.

No inbreeding is necessary to perpetuate the lutino, so it can be steadily outcrossed unless the breeder desires a lutino male. The main advantage of this mutation is that once males become available, the strain will provide self-sexing peach-faced.

Another color mutation is the *parYellow*, or *golden cherry lovebird*. The first parYellow was bred in 1954 in Japan by Mr. Masuru Iwata. Since then, intensive breeding seems to have damaged the birds genetically. A stronger stock has been produced by crossing imported birds with European and American stock.

The *pied mutation* (dominant) in its original form shows a stunning color contrast between the yellow and the green. This mutation was first bred in California in the 1960's.

The amount of pied in a single bird is dependent upon chance. A pair that is not very well marked can produce birds with coloring that is as perfect as if the offspring were from two correctly marked pieds.

Shown here is a pied mutation of the peach-faced lovebird. There are a great many color mutations of this particular species.

The *parBlue* mutation (recessive) is sea-green in appearance, with the red and peach of the face being quite dilute.

In 1963 a Dutchman, Mr. P. Habats, purchased a pair of related peach-faced lovebirds. Mr. Habats didn't know it at the time, but these two birds were split for parBlue. He refrained from looking into the nest, and when the chicks left the nest box he found that three of them were normally colored, and the other two were parBlues. This eventually became the most common mutation of all of the European lovebirds.

The *olive* mutation (dominant) is delineated in this manner: if two olive genes are present in a peach-faced lovebird, the bird is olive. If there is only one olive gene, the bird is dark green. With no olive genes, the normal green of the wild peach-faced is called light green.

The history of the olive is largely unrecorded, but we do know that it is an Australian bird. It is probable that the first examples of the olive mutation introduced into Europe were those of Dr. Romauld Burkard in 1972.

In addition to the primary color mutations of the peach-faced lovebird, there also exist combinations of the mutant colors to form new mixtures.

Some possibilities for color breeding are as follows:
1. Yellow/white x Yellow/white = 50% Yellow/white
   25% White
   25% Yellow

2. Blue/blue x Blue/blue = 50% Blue/white
   25% White
   25% Blue

3. Green/white x Green/white = 6.25% White
   6.25% Green
   6.25% Yellow
   6.25% Blue

|  |  |
|---|---|
|  | 12.50% Green/blue |
|  | 12.50% Green/yellow |
|  | 12.50% Yellow/white |
|  | 12.50% Blue/white |
|  | 25% Green/white |
| 4. Yellow x White = | 100% Yellow/white |
| 5. Blue x White = | 100% Blue/white |
| 6. Green x White = | 100% Green/white |
| 7. Green/white x White = | 25% White |
|  | 25% Blue/white |
|  | 25% Yellow/white |
|  | 25% Green/white |
| 8. Yellow x Green/yellow = | 25% Green/yellow |
|     Green/blue = | — Green/blue |
|     Green/white = | Green/white |
|  | 25% Green/Yellow |
|  | 25% Yellow |
|  | 25% Yellow/white |
| 9. Yellow/white x Blue = | 50% [ Blue/white |
|  |      Green/yellow |
|  | 50% [ Green/blue |
|  |      Green/white |
| 10. Yellow/white x Blue/white = | 25% White |
|  | 25% Blue/white |
|  | 25% Yellow/white |
|  | 25% Green/white |
| 11. Yellow Pied/blue x Blue = | 25% Yellow Pied |
|  | 25% Green/blue |

25% Blue Pied
25% Blue

12. Yellow Pied/blue x Yellow Pied/blue =
6.25% parYellow-Pied
12.50% Yellow-Pied
12.50% parYellow-Pied/blue
25% Yellow-Pied/blue
6.25% Green
6.25% Blue
12.50% Green/blue
6.25% parBlue-Pied
12.50% Blue-Pied

## HYBRIDS
The following hybrids, among others, have been produced:

*Agapornis roseicollis x A. personata fischeri*
*A. roseicollis x A. personata personata*
*A. roseicollis x A. personata lilianae*
*A. roseicollis x A. personata nigrigenis*

# 14. *Agapornis swinderniana*

**Scientific Name:** *Agapornis swinderniana* (Kuhl), 1820.
**Common Name(s):** Swindern's Lovebird; Black-collared Lovebird.
**French Name(s):** Inséperable de Van Swindern.
**German Name(s):** Grünköpfchen; Van Swinderns Unzertrennlicher.
**Dutch Name(s):** Zwartkraag-dwergpapegaai; Groenkop-agapornis.

This species is subdivided into two subspecies by some authors while other recognize three subspecies. Their natural habitat is the Congo and Gabon. Although these birds are rarely kept in captivity, we would like to include them in our book, since it is altogether possible that they may unexpectedly become popular due to their beauty. The three subspecies, which are not recognized by all ornithologists, are: *Agapornis swinderniana swinderniana, A. s. zenkeri,* and *A. s. emini,* named by Kuhl, Reichenow and Neumann respectively. *A. swinderniana* was named by Kuhl after the Dutch Professor Th. van Swindern, *A. s. zenkeri* got its name from Prof. Reichenow who named it after the discoverer, G. Zenker, while *A. s. emini* was first described by Oskar Neumann and named after Emin Pascha, the German discoverer, whose actual name was E.K.O.T. Schnitzer. *A. s. swinderniana* originated in Liberia, *A. s. zenkeri* from eastern Cameroon to the center of the Congo, while *A. s. emini* hails from the Congo as well.

**MALE AND FEMALE COLORS:** Grass green head with somewhat less bright cheeks. The underside is light green with a yellowish glow at the throat. The back is mostly green, the rump and area just above the tail is a deep blue. The tail is green with some red at the base and black at the tips. There is a black curved band that runs along the back of the neck, with a yellowish narrower band behind it which forms a vague circle around the entire neck. Their brown eyes contain a bright yellow iris. Their beaks are grayish, their feet are dark gray. They measure about 5½ inches (14 cm), and may prove to be the smallest lovebird.

OFFSPRING: The young birds do not have the black collar and the yellowish band around the neck is extremely vague. Very little is known about the offspring before they leave the nest.

In fact, very little is known about Swindern's lovebird in general. This is the only species of *Agapornis* that does not live at the edge, but rather in the thick of the forest, preferably the dense jungle. This does little to facilitate studies on them. Due to the lack of material on these lovebirds, the species may very well turn out to be much more common than already supposed. Apparently this species prefers figs above all else, although corn, grass seeds, small fruit, and the remains of insects have been found in the stomachs of shot specimens. Perhaps these birds are kept so infrequently in captivity because of their fussy appetites. After all, it is not a simple matter to provide a constant flow of wild figs and insects for them! A pair that had been held in captivity in the Congo refused to eat anything but wild figs. Yet it would appear that certain birds among them will eat rice, and they can indeed be a plague to the cultivators of rice paddies.

It is a rare thing to come across this species since they live, as already mentioned, in the dense jungle. The only time they might be seen is when they leave the forest to go searching for their beloved wild fig trees along the river banks, or for water sources. They are rowdy little parrots and their loud chirping and screeching can be heard constantly while in flight on their food searching expeditions.

This species also distinguishes itself in other ways from most dwarf parrots in that it does not have the ring around the eye and is the only species that possesses a black beak.

Very little is known about their breeding habits. It is supposed that they use convenient little nooks and that their eggs are pure white. It is a pity that this species cannot be held in an aviary, although "cannot" may be too strong a term. However, if it takes a lot of experimentation, with who knows how many victims to achieve this end, I would feel it is better to leave them in their native land. Their chances of adjusting to a new environment, menu, etc. are rather slim and, indeed, even threaten their whole existence, so I cannot imagine any bird fancier wanting to take that chance. There has been a report of a Belgian missionary, Father Hutsbout, who had a successful experience with these birds in captivity. He declared that he was unable to keep the birds alive unless he fed them a diet of wild figs. He attempted to mix these fruits with spraymillet in order to get them to eat the seed, but to no avail. They would peck at palm-nuts and peanuts, but if the figs were not provided for them to eat, they died within three or four days. Apart from this one reported incident, there have been no other accounts of success with these lovebirds in captivity. There are other attempts being made, however, and eventual success with these birds does not seem too far-fetched. Nevertheless, as previously stated, the risk involved with keeping these birds in captivity seems hardly worth taking, as it will most likely result in the demise of many birds before success is achieved.

## 15. *Agapornis taranta*

**Scientific Name:** *Agapornis taranta* (Stanley), 1814.
**Common Name(s):** Abyssinian Lovebird; Black-winged Lovebird.
**French Name(s):** Psittacula à masque rouge.
**German Names(s):** Taranta Unzertrennlicher; Tarantapapagei; Bergpapagei.
**Dutch Name:** Abessijnse agapornis.

There are two subspecies, *Agapornis taranta taranta* (Stanley) and *Agapornis taranta nana* Neumann. Both birds are pretty much the same in appearance except that the first subspecies is a little larger and the *nana* has shorter wings and a small beak. The natural habitat stretches over southern Eritrea and southwestern Ethiopia; *A. t. taranta* lives in the northern regions while *A. t. nana* inhabits the southern regions.

**MALE COLORS:** Predominantly green with a red forehead. The ring around the eye is also red. The wings are brownish-black: the short wing feathers are green. The tail is a slightly lighter green and is black tipped. The feathers just below the tail show a yellow glow, as does the curve of the wings. Rump and feathers immediately above the tail are light green, as is the entire top of the bird. The underside is light green also. The tail feathers are green, and I repeat this because the green on the tail is still lighter than that on the back. The cheeks are clearly visible through the color design. The eyes are brown, the beak is red, and the legs are gray. This species measures 6-6½ inches (15 to 16½ cm), wings 4-4¼ inches (10-10½ cm), and tail 2-2¼ inches (5-5½ cm).

**FEMALE COLORS:** Also predominantly green. She

looks exactly like the male except for her head which does not have the red coloring of the male. This enables simple sexing. Areas that are black on the male are brownish-black on the female. Sometimes the feathers under the wings are greenish in color, sometimes brownish-black.

OFFSPRING: At the time that the young birds leave the nest they look identical to their mother, except for the beak which will remain brownish-yellow until a few weeks later, when it will turn red. In young males the black markings on the wings soon become visible, as do the few red feathers that poke through on the forehead.

As we have seen elsewhere in this book, Boetticher was thinking of re-subdividing *A. roseicollis*. He wanted to do the same with *A. taranta* in 1946. He spoke of an entirely new species which he wanted to name "*Donkorella*," after "donkoro," which was the name used by the natives. However, Boetticher's idea did not materialize, and this species was given the name *taranta*, after the "Taranta Pass" in Ethiopia, which is well known for its scenic beauty. Even today there are still many of these birds living in the Taranta pass region.

This gorgeous species was not studied in the wild as much as most; in fact, most of the details that we were able to gather have come from bird fanciers. Still, we do want to give some idea as to what their life is all about in the wild. They generally live together in small groups. The nest is used as a year-round roost, making the population of this type of lovebird rather stationary. Their singing is not at all offensive, apart from the occasional little screeching notes they tend to include in their song once in a while. As mentioned earlier, if they are upset they may even give voice to it at night! Their song is soft but should not be compared to that of 'song birds.' Mostly they just chirp, although they do let out some high whistles that can be heard during their flight. They prefer the sparse woods of the highlands and sometimes can be found at a height of 6,500-9,800 feet (2,000-3,000 meters) above sea level. Consequently, they are accustomed to some cold weather and can be kept in the outside aviary even during the winter, providing there is a draft-free and dry night shelter available. It is desirable to hang a few nesting boxes in the shelter as they prefer to sleep in these. This also allows them to nap in dark little corners during the day, which they certainly like to do.

The tarantas build their nests on the plains. This species may seem rather timid, but when given proper care they can become very affectionate. *A. t. nana* does not inhabit the high plains as exclusively as does *A. t. taranta*. Research has shown *A. t. nana* to be more of a mountain bird, and seldom lines its nest with soft building materials, whereas its close relative, *A. t. taranta*, does. We find the suggestion that the natural habitats of *A. taranta* and *A. pullaria* overlap entirely possible, although crossbreeding in the wild is virtually unknown because the two species live at different altitudes. *A. pullaria* can be found up to 4,000-5,000 feet (1,200-1,500 meters) above sea level.

*Agapornis taranta* is found mainly in dry areas where evergreens grow. They can also be found in the immediate vicinity of cultivated land. The natives attempt to get rid of them by all means available to them, since their food preference is seeds, and they can do considerable damage. Due to the fact that they are very talented in maneuvering, and thereby elude the intensive hunting attempts made on them, we can be assured they will not become extinct for quite some time. The drastic temperature changes in their native region do not phase them either, which makes them ideally suited for acclimatization after they have been imported to another land. Their main food is all kinds of seeds, berries and fruit, including wild figs. As a result they can be found more often in tree tops than on the ground. It is best to imitate nature's menu for them as closely as possible. All sorts of fruit, such as sweet apples, pears, and figs are their favorites, but they also eat hemp, millet, sunflower seeds, oats, and white seed. They also seem to really like peanuts, per Mr. Beetz' article that appeared in *Vogelrevue,* No. 1, May 1963 (we refer to this article elsewhere and in more detail)—in which he writes about *A. taranta* that he reared himself: "When I

The Abyssinian lovebird is reported to be difficult to breed, yet it is a popular bird because of its tendency to become rather close to its owner after a period of time.

am home the rest of the family are invisible to him, unless they bribe him with a peanut. My sweet-beaked pet will do anything for one, cracks the shell with much noise and ambition, and then eats the nut with eyes tightly closed in utter enjoyment." Don't forget the twigs for gnawing.

The Abyssinian lovebird—perhaps that should be changed to Ethiopian lovebird—breeds in all kinds of nooks, and there are even reports that they have been found in the nests of weaver birds, such as we saw with *A. roseicollis*. It has been said that the Abyssinian lovebird is a very difficult bird to breed. Many have attempted to provide reasons for this, some of which include nervousness and sexual incompatibility. In my opinion, breeding is often prevented by an unacceptable nest size. The nests of these birds are extremely small, some measuring no more than three square inches. The nest is lined with all kinds of soft materials, transported between the feathers by some and in the beak by others. The lining is often just a rather sparse affair, consisting of little pieces, including feathers which appear, from the coloration, to have come from the male bird.

The female lays between three to six pure white eggs, which measure 17-17.9 mm x 13.6-14 mm. The eggs are laid every other day. A hen, in examining a nest site for the first time, will demonstrate a great deal of anxiety by overly dramatic flickings of her head and much tail-flaring as she peers into the nest. After a series of many retreats and advances, she finally gains enough boldness to actually enter the nest box. During these maneuvers, the male flurries about outside the box and chatters excitedly. After emerging, the hen will attempt solicitation of food from the male. The male, equally as excited as his mate, will feed the hen with such fervor that it appears he is actually pleased to have something to contribute to the nesting procedure. Only after the hen has flown from the nest will the male venture inside. In a moment, he will fly out and persue his mate. Before long, both will return to begin the entire process over again. In a day, the birds will have accepted the box as their nest, and it is now that the male will accept the responsibility of defending it against other males when his wife is inside. All hatching is done by the female, who sits on the eggs about three and a half weeks. The male takes care of feeding her. Once the young have hatched out of the eggs both parents take care of feeding them, though this becomes primarily the male's job once they have flown out of the nest. The fledglings are about six to seven weeks old when they leave the nesting box.

A hen defending her nest is an extremely formidable opponent. She situates herself within the nest in such a manner that her body is protected by the bulk of the nest, and only her head projects from the hole. The offensive hen is unwilling to go into the nest unless she has first painstakingly inspected the interior. This is quite impossible if the rightful owner is still in the nest. There was a case where an invading hen reached inside a nest hole and tore the hen out of her nest by her beak. In the struggle, however, the hens separated, and the rightful owner was once again inside her nest, ready to defend it against her attacker.

Beetz says: "The taranta is a bird that can become very close to his owner after a given time. Breeding results are obtained when each pair is housed separately. During the breeding time, other bird species and even fellow species are chased and attacked and can even become injured if pairs are not housed separately. It is also advisable to transport them separately; this will avoid a lot of problems.

Abyssinian lovebirds spend much time squabbling among each other even when not breeding. There are certain social 'rules,' however, which make serious fighting quite rare in roomy surroundings. This bird confines its fights to members of the same sex, for the attachment between the members of a pair is extremely strong. Also, hens are a great deal larger and stronger than the males, making actual combat between the sexes highly unlikely. When hens fight, their males stay on the sidelines, lending support to their mates by flaring their tails, chattering and lunging with the bill. The males, however, stay quite clear of the action, involving themselves instead with bickering with the other males. The hen's strength is greatest inside her nesting chamber. As she moves further away from her domain, her strength diminishes until, at about a yard from the nest, the hens are just about equal. When a hen is pursued, it flies to its nest hole, where the chase usually stops. Among Abyssinian lovebirds, it is the female who protects the male, and frequently a male bird can be observed fleeing to his wife's side for refuge.

At the time of this writing (April 7) my tarantas are sitting on a brood of five eggs. Depending upon the weather it will take 24-26 days for the chicks to hatch, which is quite a bit longer than with other dwarf parrots; the young also stay longer in the nest, namely a full six weeks. Tarantas seldom build a nest. As with the cockatiels and grass parakeets, I provide a thick layer of moist wood-shavings which I press down firmly. The nesting box measures 10 inches (25 cm) long x 6 inches (15 cm) deep x 7 inches (18 cm) high (these are inside measurements), and is fitted with a hinged lid. The opening has a diameter of 2 inches (5 cm) and is situated 1 and one-fifth inches (3 cm) from the top, off center.

The following remarks are directed at those who would like to 'finger-tame' a dwarf parrot: success is assured if one rears the young bird. Last year I took a young *A. taranta* from his nest when he was just ten days old, and placed him in a similar nesting box in my living room. For what it is worth, I would like to interject that this did not make a great deal of mess, just some extra work, since the young bird needs to be fed at regular intervals. I used a plastic eye dropper in raising my bird and reared him on a soft mixture of egg, wholemeal bread crumbs, and finely chopped lettuce, with a little lukewarm water stirred in. It should be obvious that whatever we feed a young bird must be at a constant, lukewarm temperature. The young bird became quickly accustomed to the eye dropper and promptly started screaming for food the second day when I lifted up the lid. When he started leaving the nesting box on a regular basis I placed him in a canary cage. From that day on I gave him a little dish of crushed seed (hemp, millet, and sunflower seeds). By the cage door I hung a little bath which I taped all around; this also served the purpose of providing a dark little corner to nap in, which he likes to do. They prefer to sleep in a nesting box. In the evening my taranta comes out of the cage and flies around the room. When he is tired from these excursions he comes begging me to scratch his head, and then without further ado retires into the nesting box that is reserved for him. As soon as it is light he starts talking to me in yet incomprehensible sounds, and is not satisfied until he is sitting in his cage. He is now ten months old and has achieved all adult colors. If he will ever talk with recognizable words remains to be seen. All in all I can say that the *A. taranta* is a very grateful bird. One is generously rewarded for extending good care with affection and friendship." (I wanted to include this case, since I thought it to be helpful and interesting.)

To come back to their breeding habits, there have been cases known where tarantas laid eggs in a hollow coconut. The baby birds are covered at birth by a thin layer of white down that is quite quickly replaced by one of gray; later, this in turn will be replaced by the plumage of their youth which is pretty well identical to that of the mother; the green has a more matte finish to it, while their beaks are yellowish-brown.

The chicks grow extremely slowly and still appear quite embryonic at the age of one week. For all their lack of size, however, the chicks have rather loud voices, even when they are first born. The eyes do not usually open before the chicks are at least fifteen days old, and some do not open their eyes until they reach the age of about three weeks. Do not be alarmed if one eye opens before the other, as this is quite a common occurrence among these birds. I have not seen a chick fledge before he is fifty days old.

It is advisable to separate the young from their parents once they have become adults to avoid accidents. This is not always necessary, however, for frequently this lovebird is extremely tolerant of its young, even after the offspring have passed the point of maturity. Offered as an illustration of this point is the case of a male and his two nine-month-old sons who shared the same nest box with the hen while she incubated a round of three more eggs. When the eggs hatched, all three males helped to feed the chicks, and even cared for them when the hen was away from the nest.

The first tarantas are believed to have been imported to Europe in 1906 by Italian merchants. There is some controversy with regard to the year in which success was achieved with breeding; some authors believe 1909, while others claim 1911. In 1911 there was a brood hatched in Vienna, and described in an article that appeared in *Die Gefiederte Welt*.

Young that have been born and bred in an aviary are generally not timid, which is more than can be said of many imported specimens (including those that come from Japan). If the bird keeper is calm and peaceful in his movements when in the aviary and provides proper nourishment and housing for his birds, they should quickly adjust to their new life and abode.

Abyssinian lovebirds are very peaceful and could give the impression that they might well be placed with other species in the same aviary. This is indeed possible, but only with species that are fairly aggressive; we are thinking of large birds, such as toucans, thrush-types, bulbuls, etc. Even then we shall have to keep a wary eye on them. Although sometimes it seems to work out, generally it is not a good idea to have pairs together. If one does want to experiment with this, be sure to provide sufficient nesting boxes since these are often the cause of the disagreements! The further the birds are from their nests, the less quarrelsome they become, because these birds are extremely territorial.

Sometimes out of boredom birds may start picking in each other's feathers, which is an unpleasant habit that can be "treated" by giving greens and a vitamin preparation dissolved in water. Hanging up rope(s) can also break the birds of this habit, since they like to climb up and down on them. Serving small pieces of raw meat is yet another way to overcome this problem. At any rate, this peculiar characteristic appears to cause the recipient a modicum of pain, judging by the reaction of the bird receiving this treatment. Usually, the 'picking' is restricted to the throat and forehead. Frequently, a bird will attempt an attack on some other part of the body, a move which regularly meets with disapproval from the other bird. There have been cases where the feathers of the face and lores have been almost completely stripped as a result of this action.

Serving greens presents problems too since most have been sprayed with insecticides that are too often fatal to the birds. Growing your own little garden would be ideal, but for those who cannot or do not feel so inclined take proper precautions by thoroughly washing all greens offered, such as endive, lettuce, etc., and use only the inner leaves and hearts, discarding the outer ones; this should virtually eliminate the possibility of poisoning your birds. It would appear that the constitution of the female is somewhat stronger than that of the male since the number of male deaths far outweighs that of female deaths. This holds true in the wild as well as in the aviary.

Due to the geographical location of Ethiopia (Abyssinia), this area escaped European colonization for quite some time. As a result, the Abyssinian lovebird did not enter into aviculture until much later than most other birds. When it was introduced, it came by way of the few African colonies of European powers. The first authenticated German breeding occurred in 1924, when W. Reitzig raised four offspring from as many eggs. In Britain, the first breeder was W. Lewis, who reared two in 1925. This accomplishment earned him the Avicultural Society medal. From 1925 on they were bred in France. The breeding of these birds has not really been taken seriously by many fanciers, however, because homebred stock is in constant competition with cheap imported birds.

In conclusion, these lovebirds may be somewhat timid and withdrawn at first, but are fine once they have adjusted to their surroundings. They are generally less noisy than other lovebird species and can even be kept in the home. They can be kept together with large parakeet varieties as well as with fairly aggressive birds, but not with small varieties and fellow-species, and never during the breeding period. These birds will breed just as well in a cage as in an aviary. They can be kept in an outside aviary even during the winter, although I feel that unheated available space indoors would be better. Keep in mind that lovebirds are very sensitive to being held in the hands, and catching them should be done with the utmost care.

## COLOR MUTATION

One of the strangest color mutations I have seen in *Agapornis taranta* was a sort of cinnamon color. This particular wild-caught male bird had various flight feathers that were cinnamon in coloration, the face was a paler shade of red, and the green color was dilute. The flight feathers that were usually black were now a light brown, but the underwing coverts and the secondary flight-feathers remained black.

This unique bird was probably imported in 1972 and passed through the hands of some previous owners before I acquired it. From this bird six males were bred, but no hens. The genetic make-up of this bird has remained unproved.

## HYBRIDS
*A. taranta* x *A. p. personata*
*A. taranta* x *A. p. fischeri*

The Mexican parrotlet is not as widely imported as other species of dwarf parrot, but it is still available for sale on the market.

The green-rumped parrotlet makes a good addition to a cage or aviary because of its beautiful colors and charming disposition.

# 16. Forpus Dwarf Parrots

In this chapter we will deal with the more well known dwarf parrots belonging to the genus *Forpus*. In their outward appearance they very much resemble the lovebirds, though they are not related. Apropos to this the first part of a chapter from E.N.T. Vane's book *Lovebirds and Parrotlets* is very interesting. He writes: "The only relationship that any New World parrots bear to those of the Old World is that both belong to the family *Psittacidae*. Although the parrotlets of Cental and South America are frequently known as the blue-wing lovebirds, they are not, in fact, closely allied to the true lovebirds (*Agapornis*) of Africa, but their requirements for management in captivity are very similar, as are those of other small South American parakeets, so that is is convenient to consider them with this genus."

Members of the genus *Forpus* are truly minature parrots, averaging only some five inches in length and having very short tails. Their range extends from northwest Mexico down through South America as far as northern Argentina and Paraguay. Details of the limits of the areas covered by some subspecies are rather vague owing to the lack of knowledge about the interior forests and jungles; probably there are more species waiting to be discovered yet.

Five species, further split up into some twenty subspecies, are known to science. The first is the Mexican or turquoise-rumped parrotlet, *F. cyanopygius*, of which there is three subspecies. Second is *F. passerinus*, of which there is ten subspecies accounted for, one having a turquoise rump, four having cobalt blue rumps and five having green rumps. Third, *F. sclateri* with two subspecies; these are a much darker green in body color.

Fourth, the spectacled parrotlet, *F. conspicillatus*, of which there are two sub species, with a markedly noticeable colored area around the eye which gives them their name. Lastly, *F. coelestis*, the celestial parrotlet, which is either very bright green or yellow on the head and frontal areas; again there are two subspecies.

*Forpus* parrotlets are relatively easy to keep in an aviary although I personally do not find them all that ideal as aviary birds. They are very nervous and it is entirely possible that even after a year or two in the aviary they will still fly against the wire or creep terrified into a corner with the least provocation. Use gloves if it becomes necessary to catch them for whatever reason, because they can inflict a nasty bite!

It is advisable to house each pair in their own aviary; having more than one pair in an aviary leads to friction and quarreling which certainly does not help the breeding process, which is not a simple matter to begin with. They can be placed together with lovebirds and other fellow species though. Recently imported birds need to be placed in quarantine; they must be acclimatized with the utmost care. They come from a part of the world where the weather is very mild indeed and are therefore susceptible to cold temperatures and drafts. It would be sensible to house them indoors initially. Birds that have been locally bred are a little hardier and can be kept outdoors during the winter, providing they have a very well-built, dry, and draft-free night shelter.

Their way of life is very similar to that of the lovebirds: pairs are true to each other for life, go to sleep together, and rear their brood together. Choosing a pair won't give any problems since the sexes can be readily identified: the colors of the male are darker, and he has a great deal more blue in his plumage than the female. The nesting boxes should have the following dimensions: the bottom square should measure approximately

4 and two-fifths inches (14 cm) x 4 and three-fifths inches (14 cm), the height should be 7-10 inches (18-25 cm), and the opening should be about 2 and two-fifths inches (6 cm) in diameter. The boxes should be made of hard and seasoned wood and the edges should be strengthened with metal strips. Since the species of *Forpus* do not generally use any nesting materials it might be desirable to hew a shallow hollow in the bottom where the eggs will come to lie. Complete broods vary from three to six eggs, although sometimes one might come across one consisting of eight eggs. Forget about inspecting the nests! The female will simply not tolerate this intrusion and promptly deserts her eggs. You will rarely if ever see the female during this period because she remains in the nesting box and is provided with food by her spouse. Here, too, there can be problems because if someone is near the male will not go inside the nesting box. Perhaps this is a case of forewarned is forearmed!? The breeding period is three to three and a half weeks and the young fly out when they are approximately five weeks old. Keep an eye on the female since it may happen that while she is still feeding one brood she might just "forget" that her children are still relying on her for food and start laying a new batch of eggs. In the beginning the entire brood returns to the nesting box at night to all sleep together.

Their food requirements are the same as for the lovebirds, white seed (canary seed) and millet being their main course, as well as hemp and sunflower seeds. Although they are not crazy about greens and fruit, it is nevertheless a good idea to offer these anyway. They rarely, if ever, take a water bath but do enjoy a roll in moist grass. In this connection we should provide them with a patch of grass and simply let it grow. The longer the grass, the better they like it. With a little luck one can derive much pleasure from *Forpus* parrotlets, and if one can get them to breed, so much the better.

## CELESTIAL PARROTLET
Scientific name: *Forpus coelestis coelestis* Lesson
French name: Peruche moineau à dos gris
German name: Blaugenick Sperlingspapegei
Dutch name(s): Grijsrug-dwergpapegaai, Lessons dwergpapegaai

MALE COLORS: In my opinion this is one of the most beautiful dwarf parrots. Green, in various shades, dominates here again. However, there is quite a lot of blue in his wings. The rump is also blue and there is a narrow blue band which runs along the back of his neck. His beak is grayish white, his feet are pink-red. Length: 4 and four-fifths inches (12 cm).

FEMALE COLORS: The female lacks the blue in the wings but has a blue rump and the blue "neckband," although this is much less clearly defined than in the male.

There are two subspecies of *Forpus coelestis*, namely *Forpus coelestis coelestis*, which makes its home in Ecuador and the northern part of Peru, and *Forpus coelestis xanthops*, which lives in the northeastern portion of Peru, especially in the valley of the Maranon River which is a branch of the Amazon. *F. c. xanthops* has a yellowish throat, cheeks and forehead, and more of a grayish neck.

These birds are kept quite frequently in cages in their native land and apparently breed quite readily. The same holds true for the States where they use the nesting boxes meant for parakeets. They are not imported into Europe on a large scale. According to *Avicultural Magazine*, 1964, No. 1, the first breeding results were achieved in 1963 when Mrs. Boorer of London had success with a pair that was housed in a cage equipped for breeding. The pair spent most of their time in the top of

The celestial parrotlet is frequently kept in cages and is an eager breeder, usually using the nesting box of a parakeet.

the cage so Mrs. Boorer promptly placed the feeding dish at the top also. After their arrival they only ate spraymillet but soon started to include a mixture of canary seed, mixed millets, groats and hemp. And she continues: "However, they reared their brood entirely on spraymillet. During the molt they became extremely fond of hemp and threw out all their other seed in an effort to find it. They also had cuttlefish, grit, apple (which they eat sporadically) and seeding grass, of which they were fond. Dried spinach and powdered yeast and C.L.O. were added to the seed mixture. They ignored sunflower seed, never used their feet to pick up anything, and also chewed up a lot of wood.

"When a budgerigar nest-box was placed at one end of the cage the birds remained rooted to the perch at the other end for the next ten days. The cock finally investigated the box and shortly after this the two of them used it for roosting. The hen started incubating on April 11th. . . . The eggs were white and were laid every second day. I don't know whether incubation started with the laying of the first egg but certainly the nestlings were all different sizes and when they finally flew it was at three-day intervals. . . . The cock spent much time in the nest-box but, as he could always be seen sitting just inside the entrance hole, I am certain he took no part in incubation. Seventeen days after the hen began incubation. . . a faint squeaking could be heard in the box, so I presume the first egg had hatched. Four weeks later a chick was first seen at the nest-box entrance. . . . Seven weeks after the first hatching date two nestlings were thrown out of the nest-box. The larger was a young cock, with his blue quills just showing on his wings; the smaller was completely bald. I replaced these, and an hour later the young cock was again ejected, this time with both legs bleeding. . . . Shortly after this the mummified remains of another young cock was found on the cage floor. On June 23rd, eight weeks after hatching, the first young hen flew, to be followed at three-day intervals by three others. The fourth hen had been attacked in the nest-box and had a crippled leg. As the adult hen was chivying them, the fledglings were removed to a separate cage on the morning that the last one flew. Once they had left the nest the youngsters were entirely self-supporting. The parents were never seen to feed them. . . . There was also a large amount of millet and millet husks (in the nest-box) suggesting that the parents had been carrying whole millet into the box for some time before the fledglings flew."

As far as the birds' behavior is concerned, Mrs. Boorer stated: "The pair I possess are rather silent, shy birds. They are extremely reluctant to come to the floor of the cage and like all their food hung up high. They have never bathed and dislike being sprayed. They roost very early; even in midsummer they have disappeared into their box by six o'clock. Perhaps the most noticeable feature is that the birds are always together. They are also very alert and suspicious and the slightest unusual sound causes them to draw themselves up very erect on the perch and peer around in all directions until they have located its origin.

"If one flies, the other immediately follows. They sit pressed together on the perch and spend much time in mutual preening. When I had to remove the hen, who became ill, they called to each other for several hours. When they do disagree they make a high-pitched chattering, drawing themselves up very erect with feathers tight. Their heads bob and weave and feint with their beaks open. The leg nearest their opponent is raised and makes vague grasping movements in the air. I have never seen them touch each other during this display, which usually ends by one bird leaving the perch to fly round to the other side of the one left. Their threat display is rather impressive. With all feathers fluffed out and beaks open, they rock very slowly backwards. When it seems they are about to fall off their perch, they lunge forward extremely fast. This is done silently and the strike forward is made long before the object they are threatening is within range. I have never seen them do this to each other. It seems to be directed solely to external dangers."

## GUIANA PARROTLET

Scientific name: *Forpus passerinus* Linnaeus
French name: Perruche moineau de Guyana
German name: Grünbürzeliger Sperling-Papagei
Dutch name(s): Groenstuit-dwergpapegaaitje, Guyana-dwergpapegaai

There are according to Vane some eleven subspecies. The race *F. p. olallae* was named only comparatively recently and is not mentioned in Peters' *Check List*. All parrotlets live on the north coast of South America to northern Argentina. They are:

**Ceara Dwarf Parrotlet or Brazilian Blue-winged Dwarf Parrotlet** *(Forpus passerinus flavissimus* Hellmayr)

These parrotlets live in the northeastern regions of Brazil and are quite concentrated in the state of Ceara. They look quite a lot like *F. p. vividus* although they are somewhat lighter green and their foreheads are more of a yellowish-green. Rutgers' *Encyclopedia* states that the first successful crossing took place in 1950 between the Ceara and the *passerinus* in Odense, Denmark. There were two pairs housed in breeding cages having nesting

There are eleven subspecies of the Guiana parrotlet, a beautiful dwarf parrot that is native to South America.

boxes attached to the outside. The two pairs reared nine offspring between them and the remarkable thing about it all was that the males resembled the father, while the females resembled the mother!

### Delicate Parrotlet (*Forpus passerinus deliciosus* Ridgway)

This subspecies is the smallest of the *passerinus* types. This type falls somewhere in between the blue parrotlets and the group with the green rump and feathers immediately above the rump. The rump of this species is green along with the above-the-tail feathers, but shows a turquoise glow as well which gives a lovely effect. No doubt this is one of the most beautiful birds in this group. The plumage is shinier than that of the Guyana dwarf parrotlet and the color of the wings is a deeper blue. The rapids area of the Amazon comprises the natural territory of this species. Unfortunately, there are not very many of them offered on the market.

### Guyana Dwarf Parrotlet (*Forpus passerinus passerinus* Linnaeus)

MALE COLORS: Primarily green, duller at the back of the neck. The cheeks, rump and tail are grass green, the underside yellowish-green. At the edge of the wings and on the shorter wing feathers there is quite a bit of blue as in the feathers underneath the wings. The beak is grayish white, the feet are flesh-colored, and the eyes are brown. This species measures about 4 and four-fifths inches (12 cm).

FEMALE COLORS: The colors are less bright and the blue is missing altogether. The underside is lighter in color.

OFFSPRING: These look much like the mother but soon the males will begin to show the blue in their plumage.

This adorable parrotlet lives in Surinam, Guyana and neighboring French Guiana. Many of the natives keep them in cages in their houses after having taken them out of their nest and hand-feeding them, which explains why those particular specimens are so tame. Except for the breeding period, these goregeous but quiet birds roam around in large groups searching for food, which consists of various seeds, berries, and fruit. Their chirping and soft chatter make one think of a group of cackling sparrows. In the aviary one should offer millet, white seed, spraymillets, hemp, and cracked sunflower seeds, which they love. Although they are not crazy about greens, these should be offered as well as fruit (apples, pears, bananas and such) although some of them may not even give these a second glance! During the breeding period we should offer old white bread soaked in milk. As soon as the breeding period has arrived, the various pairs go off by themselves to look for a suitable place where they lay their white eggs without the benefit of any nest material. The number of eggs varies quite a bit; the Penard egg collection housed in the Rijksmuseum of Natural History in Leiden (Netherlands) shows a brood of 2 eggs and one of 5 eggs. In aviaries the number can vary even more since as much as nine eggs have been laid in one batch. All the hatching is done by the female and takes about three weeks, during which time the male provides her with food. The offspring stay in the nesting box for thirty to forty-five days, but even after they have flown out they will still be fed by the parents for a short time to follow. During this period it might behoove one to keep an eye on the male since it is not all that unusual for him to start feather plucking his chicks, or worse, he may even kill them. In such a case he should be removed from the aviary and the female will take care of whatever is left. (Remember to wear gloves in the event you need to catch any of the birds.)

The best breeding results are obtained when each pair is given its own abode where they can go about their business undisturbed. Normally this subspecies gets along very well with other birds but during the breeding period there seems to be a change of heart. They can become quite aggressive at that time and will aim for the little feet of their fellow inmates.

As far as I know cross-breeding has been achieved with the blue-winged and blue-necked dwarf parrotlets.

These birds are very sensitive to both drafts and moisture. We should also ensure that the food we serve them is not too wet, and in addition provide them with some variety: greens, fruit (apples, pears, berries, plums, pineapple, bananas and such) millet, plenty of oats, and very little hemp in addition to the regular seed menu, as mentioned earlier.

During the winter months, of course, the birds should be housed inside in roomy cages placed in a heated area.

## Hacha Dwarf Parrotlet (*Forpus passerinus cyanophanes* Todd)

This beautiful bird, which is distinguished from the other subspecies by the brighter blue color on the wings, rump and plumage immediately above the rump, lives in the tropical parts of northeastern Colombia (east of the Santa Marta Mountains). There are specimens kept in the United States but not, to my knowledge, in Europe.

## Hartlaub's Dwarf Parrotlet (*Forpus passerinus cyanochlorus* Schlegel )

The rump and plumage immediately above it are green, as is the case with the Venezuelan green-rumped parrotlet. However, the beak is smaller and the underside of the female is a brighter yellowish-green. This bird is rarely offered on the market in Europe, which is a shame. In the States, of course, they are far more common. Their habitat includes northwestern Brazil, particularly around the river basin of the Negro (Rio Branco).

**Large-billed Parrotlet** (*Forpus passerinus crassirostris* Taczanowski)

This parrotlet inhabits the northeastern regions of Peru, extreme southeastern Colombia, and northwestern Brazil. The ranges of this subspecies as well as those to follow overlap each other. However, I do not know whether any of these subspecies cross-breed. Their coloring is primarily green, but darkest on the forehead. Their wings and rump are blue; under the wings they are light blue. The females do not possess the blue colors and their foreheads are duller in color. Although these birds are quite popular in the States very few of them are exported to Europe.

**Ridgway's Blue Winged Dwarf Parrotlet or Blue Winged Dwarf Parrotlet** (*Forpus passerinus vividus* Ridgway)

This species used to be known as *Forpus passerinus passerinus*, which is the third subspecies listed. This parrotlet inhabits Bahia in the eastern part of Brazil.

MALE COLORS: Primarily green; the small wing feathers, the rump and the curve of the wings are a beautiful bright blue. The cheeks and underparts are lighter green than the rest of the body. Eyes are brown, the feet are brownish-gray, and the beak is grayish-white. This species measures about 4 and two-fifths inches (11 cm).

FEMALE COLORS: The female's plumage has no blue in it. Her rump is bright green and her forehead is a yellowish color. On some females this yellowish color continues downward to include the sides of the head.

Under the wings she is green, whereas the male is blue.

OFFSPRING: These look much like the female, but the young males will soon start to show the blue in their plumage. These parrotlets live in large groups and like to roam around the edge of woods and jungles and by the river banks. They are very concentrated near the rapids of the Rio Grande, which is a branch of the Sao Francisco River in western Bahia. I noticed that they feast on all sorts of weed seeds there as well as wild "paradise-apples" and twigs of the "gourd" trees.

These birds are very popular with aviary keepers, since they get along wonderfully well with all kinds of birds except for parrot types! Breeding results are often achieved in the aviary although success has also been gained in a roomy cage. I don't feel that a cage is the proper place for them, but they are magnificent in a nice roomy outside aviary. When the sun shines on their plumage it transforms them to bright, flying jewels—indeed a pleasure to behold! As is the case with the other *Forpus* species, these birds need to be acclimatized with the utmost care. They must be kept indoors at least six months (and a few more would be preferable) before being placed outside. When the breeding time draws near the various couples go off by themselves to select a suitable nesting place, which is often a hole in a tree, although broods have been found in the old nests of oven birds. The first to report this was Azara in *Voyages dans l'Amerique meridionale* (1809), although many ornithologists doubted the authenticity of his claim. In 1903, however, the "Academie der Wissenschaften" of Vienna sent an expedition to northeastern Brazil. Otmar Reiser compiled the ornithological research data gained from this expedition which revealed that they, too, had found a nest containing three eggs in an old oven bird loam nest. The dull, white eggs were found lying on a layer of rags, duck feathers, and a number of small green feathers from the mother.

They eat the same food as lovebirds and their breeding habits and related data were already discussed at the beginning of this chapter.

### Salvadori's Dwarf Parrotlet *(Forpus passerinus flavescens* Salvadori)

Here again is a bird that is bred in the United States by bird fanciers but very little, if at all, in Europe. This subspecies' natural habitat is in eastern Bolivia and in southeastern and centraleastern Peru. I know very little about their living habits. Although green is a dominating color in all *Forpus* species, in this particular subspecies this color is very light, almost yellow; the wings and rump are a dull blue. The beak is off-white and the feet are flesh-colored.

### Spengel's Dwarf Parrotlet *(Forpus passerinus spengeli* Hartlaub)

This subspecies lives in the northern part of Colombia (Santa Marta Mountains at Atlantico) and is regularly exported to various parts of the world. In 1957 in England this bird was cross-bred with *Forpus passerinus passerinus* and the same breeder reported success with the first breeding the following year. This lovely bird looks a lot like *Forpus cyanopygius*, including the turquoise rump. However, they are somewhat smaller and have a considerably sturdier beak which is slightly flattened at the sides.

### Venezuelan Green-Rumped Parrotlet *(Forpus passerinus viridissimus* Lafresnaye)

Northern Venezuela is the natural habitat of this parrotlet which has much in common with the Guyana dwarf parrotlet, although that bird is a little lighter in build. It is only sporadically exported. In 1868 this bird was spotted in Curacao and described by G.J. Simons in his *Description of the Island of Curacao*. Nothing further was published about this subspecies until 1943 when M. de Jong (a Dutch author of a few books on European birds) was able to catch an exhausted specimen that landed on the wall of the Waterfort in Willemstad. Apparently this bird had flown over from Venezuela. Personally, I feel we are dealing here with a very interesting ornithological question: have enough of these birds found their way to Curacao in the course of time so that this subspecies has a breeding population there? According to de Jong more of these birds can be spotted on the island, but there is some question as to whether these are just a few individual specimens that have flown over from Venezuela, or whether these are offspring from a group of forty that were imported in 1940 and given free reign on the plantation "Klein Piscadera." Simons calls this bird "bibitji", but the people from Curacao refer to it as "bibitu". This bird is a good choice for keeping in an aviary: it is both beautifully colored and charmingly dispositioned.

### Gyldenstolpe's Parrotlet *(Forpus passerinus olallae* Gyldenstolpe)

This bird is a subspecies of the species *passerinus*. It could well be mistaken for the large-billed parrotlet *(Forpus passerinus crassirostris)* except for the fact that the rump and feathers immediately above the tail are even darker in color. The blue on the wings is not obvious. Many of the greens are darker. The beak is white but ends in a dark point. They live in West Brazil, particularly in the Amazon area.

## MEXICAN PARROTLET or TURQUOISE-RUMPED PARROTLET

Scientific name: *Forpus cyanopygius* Souance
French name: Perruche à croupion bleu
German name(s): Heller Sperling-Papagei, Blaubürzel-Sperling-Papagei
Dutch name: Mexicaans dwergpapegaai.

There are three subspecies of *Forpus cyanopygius*, namely *Forpus cyanopygius lutescens* Van Rossem, from west Mexico, *Forpus cyanopygius cyanopygius* (Souance), from the Islas Tres Marias, an island group off the west coast of Mexico, and finally *Forpus cyanopygius pallidus* from northwestern Mexico, Sonora and bordering areas. The last subspecies was named by Brewster. All three subspecies vary very little from each other, both in color as well as size. In older literature *F.c. cyanopygius* was called *F.c. insularis* and *F.c. lutescens* was called *F.c. cyanopygius*, but the above names are now considered correct.

MALE COLORS: Primarily green, the underside is more of a yellowish green, as are the cheeks and forehead. Some of the feathers above the rump and the rump itself are turquoise in color; the short wing feathers are dark blue while the long ones are a dull dark green; the feathers underneath the wing are green and blue. The beak is grayish white, the eyes are yellowish brown, and the feet are a gray-brown.

FEMALE COLORS: The female has less blue in her plumage; her wings, including the short wing feathers, are green.

OFFSPRING: By the time they have flown out of the nest they look a lot like the adult female. Soon, however, the males can be recognized because of the blue under their wings, as well as their bluish rumps.

These parrotlets are not much larger than your everyday house-and-garden variety sparrow. They are not

The first breeding results of the Mexican parrotlet were reported in Britain, many years ago; since then, many other successful breeding attempts have occurred.

imported as much as most species but nevertheless are available for sale on the market. Sometimes a few of them may even get mixed up with a shipment of a different species with which they have much in common. An expert, however, will look for the turquoise rump which is a trademark of *F. cyanopygius*. The first breeding results were reported from Britain in 1927. The pair concerned bred in a nesting box that was really meant for lovebirds. Of course, soon after many other breeding results took place. Cross-breeding has been achieved with *Forpus coelestis* and *Forpus conspicillatus*.


## SCLATER'S PARROTLET
Scientific name: *Forpus sclateri* G.R. Gray
French name: Perruche moineau de Sclater
German name: Sclater's Sperlimgspapagei
Dutch name: Sclater's dwerpapegaai

MALE COLORS: This bird is the most green of all the *Forpus* species. The top of this bird is dark green while the under parts are somewhat lighter. The forehead and cheeks are also a lighter tone of green. There is quite a lot of blue in the wings, including underneath. The top part of the beak is a little darker than the bottom half. They measure 4 and 2/5 inches. (11 cm).

FEMALE COLORS: The female is somewhat smaller than the male, has no blue in her plumage, and the coloring of her head leans more towards a yellowish tint.


## SPECTACLED PARROTLET
Scientific name: *Forpus conspicillatus* (Lafresnaye)
French name: Perruch moineau à lunettes
German name: Augenring-Sperlingspapagei
Dutch name: Bril-dwergpapegaai

MALE COLORS: Primarily green in color, the head is grass green, the underside is green with a bluish glow. There is a lot of blue on the wings and the rump is sky blue. They get their name from the blue ring around their eyes. The beak is off-white, the feet are pink. They measure 4 and 2/5 inches (11 cm).

FEMALE COLORS: There is no blue in her plumage. Her green coloring is brighter than that of the male.

OFFSPRING: Look like the female. The blue in the males does not begin to appear until quite late.

This small parrotlet makes its home in Colombia. There is a further subspecies, *F.c. caucae*, which lives in the western part of that country. In the States this parrotlet is reasonably common, kept in both aviaries and cages. They are rarely seen in Europe. They are certainly worthwhile birds to keep.

The first breeding results in captivity were reported from California, Cross-breeding was successfully achieved with *F.p. vividus*. The care and feeding of this bird parallel that of the blue-winged dwarf parrotlet.

The uppermost bird is a vernal hanging parrot, and the lowermost bird is a blue-crowned hanging parrot. These birds sleep in an inverted position, hence the name "hanging parrot."

# 17. Hanging Parrots (*Loriculus* Blyth)

These comical birds, which sleep hanging upside down like bats, measure between 4 and 6½ inches (10-16 cm), so can be kept even by those fanciers who have only limited space available. These birds may even be hanging upside down while taking care of their natural bodily functions, which can come as a nasty, wet surprise to the unaware vistor who stands too close to the wire! Their beaks are slender and look a little like that of the genus *Trichoglossus*. Depending upon the species the beak is either red or black. Their wings are sleek and long but their tails are surprisingly short. They are great acrobats and trapeze artists taking full advantage of the talents of their beaks; in fact, they rarely have their feet on the ground. Consequently, it is important to provide them with a variable gym consisting of all sorts of climbing bars. They are active birds and chatter constantly. It would be difficult not to be affected by their charm. Keeping hanging parrakeets can give the fancier a great deal of pleasure indeed. Unfortunately, however, they are not able to stay outdoors during the winter; in fact, a lightly heated area is to be recommended. The flight of these birds is reported to be much like that of the finches in that it involves rapid beating of the wings broken at intervals by short pauses with closed wings.

They like to eat all sorts of seeds (oats, millet, white seed, hemp, etc.), insects ("ant eggs," meal worms, little spiders and larvae), fruit, and honey water. Fruit is the most important element of their diet with greens coming in a close second, and then willow twigs, cuttle bone, and grit. Hanging parrots build nests and transport willow twigs and elderberry twigs in between the rump and wing feathers like the *Agapornis* species. A roomy nesting box made of beachwood, like the kind we provide for grass parrakeets, is ideal. It is advisable to keep these boxes in the aviary year round as they like to go inside them when the weather is cold and wet. For fanciers who keep these charming birds indoors, nesting boxes do not need to be provided until a few weeks prior to the start of the breeding season. The boxes should be roomy since they often like to hang upside down while taking a little nap! A perch 2 inches (5 cm) down from the roof of the box will be much used by them. During the winter my hanging parrots would often disappear into the nesting box quite early in the evening and I would not see them again until morning.

Several fanciers are under the impression that hanging parrots are not particularly sociable birds. My opinion is that the contrary is true. I have kept them with other hook-beaked birds and several varieties of exotic species; I have yet to have a problem with them. It is a horse of a different color, however, where their own species are concerned! It is advisable, therefore, to keep but one pair per aviary. Providing you offer enough willow, elderberry and fruit tree twigs, the Loriculini group of birds will not destroy the greenery you have planted in the aviary—which is another definite plus for these birds. Although the sexes can generally be determined by small differences in coloring and markings, it would be preferable to go to a trusted source when purchasing these birds. In any event, a written agreement that is signed and dated which will allow us to exchange one of our birds would be best, to ensure that we will not have any problems should it turn out that we do not possess a true pair but rather two birds of the same sex.

The female lays two to four white eggs which take 22-23 days to hatch.

## BLUE-CROWNED HANGING PARROT
Scientific name: *Loriculus galgulus* (Linnaeus) 1758
French name: Loricule à tête bleue
German name: Blaukrönchen
Dutch name: Blauwkroontje
NATIVE LANDS: Malacca and Indonesia.
COLORING: Primarily green; the male has a blue blotch on his head; on his green back there is a yellowish glow. Throat, rump and feathers just above the tail are red. The beak is black and the top half extends quite a lot over the bottom half. The female lacks the blue on the head and the red throat. Length: 5 inches (13 cm).

As the name indicates, this bird sleeps in an inverted, hanging position like all others of its kind. However, when the males of this particular species are at rest, they are sometimes heard to twitter a soft yet distant song. Also, males, whether perching or resting, will usually hold their wings considerably lower than the females, thereby showing off a noticeable red stripe on the back.

## CEYLON HANGING PARROT
Scientific name: *Loriculus beryllinus* (J.R. Forster) 1781
French name: Loricule de Ceylon
German name: Blumenpapageichen
Dutch name(s): Ceylon-Hangparkiet, Bloemenpapegaaitje
NATIVE LAND: Ceylon.
COLORING: Green, with a red blotch on the head. Bright blue throat, red beak, dark red rump and feathers just above the tail. The female lacks the blotch on the throat, but she does have a marking of sorts in

that the green feathers at the throat are somewhat darker. The same applies to the cheeks. There is some red in the center of her head.

The Ceylon hanging parrot is reported to breed in the first half of the year, and occasionally again in July to September. In courting the female, the male will usually strut along the perch, holding his beak high, puffing his throat-feathers, and spreading his tail. The scarlet rump feathers will be raised and spread while he emits a squeaking warble, interspersed with the twit of the contact call.

The nest is usually a long, narrow area with a small opening for an entrance near the top. It is in this space that the hen will build her nest, which is generally made of strips nibbled from the edges of green leaves. The strips are transported in the red feathers of the rump.

## FLORES HANGING PARROT
Scientific name: *Loriculus flosculus* Wallace
French name: Loricule Lilliput
German name: Fledermauspapagei von Flores
Dutch name: Bloesemhangparkiet

NATIVE LANDS: Flores and north and southeastern Celebes.

COLORING: Green; there is a yellowish glow on the belly and a blue reflection on the throat. Red blotch present on the throat; the neck is yellowish-orange; rump and feathers just above the tail are red; the tail is blue underneath. The beak is red. Male and female are identical in coloring and markings. Fledglings do not show the red blotch on the throat until after their first molting. The beaks take quite a while before they turn from brown to red. Length 5 inches (13 cm).

Practically nothing is known about this bird and evidence of its existence cannot even be supplied.

## GOLDEN-FRONTED HANGING PARROT
Scientific name: *Loriculus aurantiifrons* Schlegel
French name: Loricule à front d'or
German name: Goldstirn-papageichen
Dutch name: Goudvoorhoofd Hangparkiet

NATIVE LANDS: New Guinea and surrounding islands.

COLORING: Green. The male has a golden yellow front while that of the female is blue. She also has blue cheeks. The male has a red blotch on the throat as well as a red rump and feathers just above the tail. The beak is black. Length 5 inches (13 cm).

There are four subspecies that inhabit the islands of Misol, Fergusson, and Goodenough, as well as the Bismarck Archipelago, New Guinea and Waigeo.

There is not information available at this time regarding the habits or feeding needs of this bird. Its distribution would seem to verify the theory that it is primarily a lowland species.


## MOLUCCAN HANGING PARROT
Scientific name: *Loriculus amabilis* Wallace
French name: Loricule aimable
German name: Zierpapagei
Dutch name: Halmaherahangparkiet

NATIVE LANDS: Sula Islands, Large Sangir Islands, and the Islands of Pelling, Banggai, Halmahera and Batjan.

COLORING: Red head, green forehead, red blotch on the throat and just above the tail; green underneath the tail, red rump, green back. The female lacks the red on the head. The beak is black.

Ornithologists recognize four subspecies that inhabit the regions already mentioned. They are so closely related to the Philippine hanging parrakeet, however, that one would need to be quite expert to be able to distinguish the small differences between them. Length about 5 inches (13 cm).


## PHILIPPINE HANGING PARROT
Scientific name: *Loriculus philippensis* (Muller)
French name: Loricule des Philippines
German name: Rotkäppchen
Dutch name: Philippijnse Hangparkiet
  NATIVE LANDS: Philippines.
  COLORING: Green. The male has a red blotch on the forehead and a red markings on the throat. The female lacks both of these markings. The male's cheeks are green, while the female's are blue. The green head has a yellowish glow. There is a golden blotch on the neck. The beak is red. Length 5 inches (13 cm).

Ornithologists recognize eleven subspecies, all of which vary somewhat by small differences in coloring. They are widely kept in cages and aviaries in their native land and are fortunately becoming more and more available abroad. They are ideal aviary birds for the fancier who does not mind taking a little extra care of his birds. They are generally healthy birds and not very demanding where weather conditions are concerned. This species was first imported into Europe 1875.

In appearance, this bird is much closer to a finch than the vernal and blue-crowned hanging parrots. They are also much less dextrous with their feet when they are feeding, only using the toes to steady the food, not to actually hold it. They will bathe in standing water, but it appears that they prefer foliage and rain baths.


## RED-CAPPED PARROT
Scientific name: *Loriculus stigmatus* (S. Muller)

French name: Loriculus à tête rouge
German name: Rotplättchen
Dutch name: Celebes Hangparkiet

NATIVE LANDS: Celebes, Togia Islands, Muna and Buton Islands.

COLORING: Green; the male has a red "cap" and a red blotch on the throat. He also shows red on the tail, the feathers just above the tail, and the edge of the wings; the female is green in all these places. The beak is black and there is some yellow on the back. Length 5 inches (13 cm).

All that is known about their breeding habits is that they breed twice a year, in February and August. The courting procedure is not really described except for the fact that the male will vibrate his tail rapidly when peering inside the nest box.


**VERNAL HANGING PARROT**
Scientific name: *Loriculus vernalis* (Sparrman)
French name: Loricule des Indes
German name: Fruhlingspapageichen
Dutch name: Lentepapegaaitje

NATIVE LANDS: India to Vietnam.

COLORING: Mostly green, brighter on the head. There is a blotch on the throat which is a darker shade of sky blue. The rump is rust colored as are the feathers just above the tail. The tail is blue underneath. The female lacks the blotch on the throat. The beak is red. Length: 5-5½ inches (13-14 cm).

This bird is rather difficult to locate in the wild because its plumage blends so well with the surrounding foliage. Only when an entire flock suddenly takes flight can they be observed with any ease. The birds are quite gentle and are not easily upset by onlookers.

In the wild, the vernal hanging parrot is reported to

breed between January and April, but in captivity their breeding period continues on well past this limited period of time. It is possible that this is a result of better nutrition provided by bird keepers. In the wild, proper foodstuffs are most likely seasonal.

## YELLOW-THROATED HANGING PARROT
Scientific name: *Loriculus pusillus* G.R. Gray
French name: Loricule à gorge jaune
German name: Elfenpapageichen
Dutch name: Javaanse Hangparkiet
 NATIVE LANDS: Java and Bali.
 COLORING: Green with a deep yellow reflection on the back. There is a large golden blotch on the throat. The rump is dark red as are the feathers just above the tail. The beak is red; the tail feathers are red underneath, but the inside seams are sky blue. The female lacks the yellow colors on the back and throat. Length 4¾ and 5½ inches (12-14 cm).

These birds are well-camouflaged in the trees of their environment because of their color and size. Their breeding habits are much like those of the Ceylon hanging parrot.

# 18. Fig Parrots (*Opopsitta* Sclater)

The genus *Opopsitta* has two species and numerous subspecies. Generally known as fig parrots, these birds range over the western Pacific area, from eastern Indonesia to New South Wales. They are available at least occasionally on the market, and their beauty certainly warrants our attention.

They are very peaceful and quiet birds both in the wild and in captivity, making very little noise while they are feeding, and consequently rather difficult to spot in the foliage. However, when someone gets too close to them they let out high pitched whistling sounds as in warning of danger. When the evening comes they leave the trees upon which they feed to spend the night in the eucalyptus trees in the savannas. Come sun-up they are off again to busy themselves with the business of filling their tummies! Practically nothing is known about their breeding habits. Forshaw, however, found nests in the melaenca tree, some 30 feet (9 m) up. Each of the three nests that he found contained two white eggs.

**Double-Eyed Fig Parrot**
Scientific name: *Opopsitta diophthalma* (Hombron & Jacquinot)
French name: Lorillet a double oeil
German name: Maskenzweipapagei
Dutch name: Blauwoordwergpapegaai

There are some six subspecies that live in New Guinea and three that live in Australia, namely *O. d. macleayana, O. d. aruensis, O. d. coccineifrons, O. d.*

*coxeni, O. d. festetichi, O. d. inseparabilis, O. d. marshalli* and *O. d. diophthalma.*

**COLORING:** *Opopsitta diophthalma diophthalma* has a red forehead and cheeks and is orange starting at the crown going towards the back of the head. There is a small purple band bordering the back part of the crown. There is a curved line of bright blue feathers over the eyes. The beak is silver gray turning to black towards its end. Length 4¾ inches (12 cm).

**NATIVE LANDS:** Western Papua, Misool and Salawati.

This subspecies is an excellent cage or aviary bird, and has a high level of intelligence.

*Opopsitta d. aurensis* is another subspecies from Indonesia, Aru Islands and southern New Guinea. *O. d. marshalli*—Marshall's lorilet—that lives in Queensland and the Cape York Peninsula in Australia. This subspecies, however, is not mentioned by Peters in his *Check List of Birds of the World*, Cambridge, Massachusetts. Captain A. J. Marshall discovered this bird in 1942 and so far very few are being exported. The male has some pale red in the face and a soft purple color under the ear. There is a pale blue blotch above the eye. The skull area is a faded yellow. The female has no red in her plumage, and her head and neck are a bluish purple. Length 5½ inches (14 cm).

Several times during our three year stay in Australia my wife and I had the pleasure of seeing a large group—that is about 150-200—of these birds. They prefer to live in rain forests. They are fast fliers and constantly give voice to their shrill little cries during flight. While searching for food up in the trees they continuously communicate with each other by means of sharp whistling sounds. According to Forshaw these birds eat mold as well as fruit, as he had seen them remove it from behind the bark of trees; we have never seen this but add the notation for what it is worth. They look for holes in trees, preferably high up, in which to make their nests. They might also carve their own hollow in soft or moldy wood. The female lays two white eggs. While in Australia I did not come across any aviculturists who had any experience with this species. Considering the recent discovery of this bird, it is understandable that the Australian government is giving full protection to it; hence they are difficult, if not impossible, to come by.

*Opopsitta d. aurensis* lives—as we have seen—on the Aru Islands as well as in New Guinea. This is a very rare bird indeed both in the wild and in captivity. The males have a red forehead encircled by a yellow band. The cheeks are red also and have a thin red band that runs along underneath. The rest of their body is green. The female's cheeks are brownish instead of red.

*Opopsitta d. macleayana*—Ramsay's lorilet (also referred to as McCoy's lorilet)—inhabits the rain forests of northern Queensland. Length 6½ inches (16 cm).

This bird has a red blotch on the forehead as well as red cheeks. Around the eyes they are blue as well as where the cheeks end. The balance of their body is primarily green with yellow underneath, paler on the belly and underneath the tail. The female lacks the red on the head.

*Opopsitta d. coxeni*—Coxen's lorilet—inhabits southeastern Queensland and the northeastern part of New South Wales. This is the largest bird in this group, measuring 6¾ inches (17 cm). There are very few of these birds in captivity. In the wild they live in tiny groups of three or four, usually in pairs. Due to the constant cultivation of land that keeps infringing more and more into their natural territory these birds are being driven back into virtually impregnable regions. Their call is rather quiet, which also does not help in trying to locate them.

Their beak is black; there is some blue on the forehead and on the regions of the cheeks. They are red around the ears and there are some red feathers in the face. (My wife once said they appear to have a constant case of the measles!) The rest of their plumage is green.

**Orange-Breasted Fig Parrot**
Scientific name: *Opopsitta gulielmiterti melanogenia* (Schlegel)
French name: Lorillet Aru aux joues noires
German name(s): Goldbrustzwergpapagei, Schwarzstirniger Zwergpapagei
Dutch name: Zwartoor—Dwergpapegaai

COLORING: Green. Blue forehead, yellow throat, yellow-red crop and chest. The curve of the wing is blue. White cheeks, bordered in black; gray-black beak. Length 4¾ inches (12 cm), which is by far the smallest in the group.

Although this bird, along with the subspecies, is rarely available for purchasing, we still wish to note a few specifics. First of all, as is the case with all the other birds discussed, we need to provide plenty of fruit for them, such as figs (these being their favorites, as is indicated by their name), dates, grapes, pears, bananas, etc. Instead of ordinary water we should give them honey water. Seed, grit, and small pieces of charcoal should not be missing from the menu.

There are seven subspecies which vary only in small coloring differences. They are seldom seen in captivity: *Opopsitta g. gulielmiterti* from Salawati and the coast directly opposite, in West Iran (Vogelkop).
*Opopsitta gulielmiterti melanogenia* from the Aru Islands, Indonesia.
*Opopsitta gulielmiterti nigrifrons* from the northern

part of New Guinea as is *O. g. ramuensis* (Ramu River).
*Opopsitta g. amabilis* from northeastern New Guinea (from Huon Peninsula east to Milne Bay).
*Opopsitta g. fuscifrons* from the Snow Mountains and the Orange area.
*Opopsitta g. suavissima* from the southern coast of southwestern New Guinea.

The scientific name of the genus *Opopsitta* is really a spelling error and was supposed to have been *Cyclopsitta*, with "*cyclops*" meaning "with the round face," and "*psitta*" meaning "parrot," "*duo*" meaning "two" and "*ophthalmos*" meaning "eye."

The genus *Micropsitta* has six species and fourteen subspecies. These are known as the pigmy parrots, being very small birds. Due to their size they are in great demand, and the more specialized bird breeder may yearly offer a few specimens for sale. Many of these birds are no larger than a gray waxbill or zebra finch. These species live on the Solomon Islands, New Guinea, and many other islands in this general vicinity. They are quite difficult to keep in captivity since their constitution is far from hardy. They eat termites, "ant eggs," fungus, and mushrooms. Since they are hard to come by I see little point in naming all of the species and subspecies.

Dr. S. Bergmann, a Swedish biologist, made two expeditions to New Guinea a few years back with the permission of the Dutch Government and gathered numerous data on these birds. They make their nests in termite nests and are located high up in trees. The termites, however, completely close off the passage opening between the termite nest and the bird's breeding area. Both parties seem to find this a suitable arrangement. Besides termites these birds also eat a white substance, as yet not scientifically defined, that oozes from certain trees; perhaps it comes from mold. Older chicks and new eggs are watched over simultaneously and at night these older young are fed from the crop of the father! This is a most unique occurrence in the bird world.

## Bibliography

Adlersparre, A., Dimorphismus des Jugenkleides und Nestbau bei *Agapornis*. J. Ornith. 86, 248, 1938.
Allen, William, Halfmoons and Dwarf Parrots. Neptune, 1967.
Arnall, L. and I.F. Keymer, Bird Diseases. Neptune, 1975.
Austin, O.L.Jr., Birds of the World. New York, 1961.
Dilger, William C., The Comparative Ethology of the African Parrot Genus *Agapornis*. Z. Tierpsychologie 17, 649-653, 667-683, 684-685, 1960.
Dilger, William C., Studies in *Agapornis*. Avic. Mag. 64, 91, 1958.
Forshaw, J., Parrots of the World, Neptune, 1977
Hampe, H., The nesting habits of *Agapornis pullaria*. Avic. Mag. 2, 148, 1937.
Hampe, H., Die Unzertrennlichen. Pfungstadt, 1957.
Luke, L.P., Lovebirds and Parrotlets. London, 1956.
Neunzig, K., Fremdlandische Stubenvogel. Amsterdam, 1965.
Perry, J., Breeding the Red-faced Lovebird *(Agapornis pullaria)* in South Africa. Avic. Mag. 65, 119, 1959.
Peters, J.L., Check-list of Birds of the World, Vol. 3 Cambridge, 1937.
Soderberg, P.M., All About Lovebirds. Neptune, 1977
Vane, E.N.T., Guide to Lovebirds and Parrotlets. London, 1958.
Vriends, M., Agapornissen en andere Dwergpapegaaien. Wageningen, 1972/1978.
Vriends, M., Das grosse Buch der Vogel in Kafig und Voliere. Munchen, 1976.
Vriends, M., Het Sierparkietenboek. Amsterdam, 1974.
Vriends, M., Prisma Papegaaienboek. Utrecht, 1977.
Vriends, M., Zuidamerikaanse Parkieten. Zutphen, 1978.
Witt, Clifton R., Black Masks In Your Basement. The A.F.A. watchbird, Volume V, nr. 1, 1978.

# PHOTO INDEX

Abyssinian; 68, 76, 176, 209
Aviary; 29, 30, 34
  maintenance of; 40
  Birdroom; 32, 37
Black-cheeked lovebird; 142, 145, 184, 185
Black-collared lovebird; 73
Blue-crowned hanging parrot; 72, 238
Cages; 12, 34, 43
Celestial parrotlet; 223
Eggs; 57
Electric lighting; 38
Equipment, cage and aviary; 42, 103
Fischer's lovebird; 8, 11, 77, 128
  mutation; (yellow); 85
Foods; 90, 97, 99
Green-rumped parrotlet; 218
Guiana parrotlet; 226
Madagascar lovebird; 72, 180, 181
Masked lovebird; 8, 54, 64, 65, 69, 148, 151
  mutation (blue); 92, 177
Medicine; 107, 111
Mexican parrotlet; 218, 235
Minerals; 45
Moscow bird market; 13, 18, 19

Nest boxes; 48, 50
Nyasaland lovebird; 84, 136
Peach-faced lovebird; 26, 47, 49, 53, 58, 79, 83, 88, 96, 164, 165, 173, 183, 188, 189, 192, 195
  bathing; 101
  chicks; 60-61
  color mutations;
    albino; 93, 169, 177
    blue; 84
    cherryhead; 89
    golden cherry; 73, 93, 169, 177
    green pied; 85, 96, 172
    modification; 184
    pied; 199
    silver; 92, 168
  comparison of young vs. mature; 178
  examination of; 20, 23
  feather plucking; 109
  hand feeding; 90, 98
  preening; 6, 17
  taming and training; 21
Philippine hanging parrot; 80-81
Red-headed lovebird; 68
Vernal hanging parrot; 72, 238
Wing-clipping; 166

# Index

Abyssinian lovebird, 20; 206
Acclimatization, 24; 25
   Madagascar, 117
   Masked, 150
   Red-headed, 166
*Agapornis*
   *cana*, 15; 112
   *personata fischeri*, 16; 124
   *personata lilianae*, 16; 135
   *personata nigrigenis*, 16; 22; 141
   *personata personata*, 147
   *pullaria*, 15; 159
   *roseicollis*, 16; 21; 174
   *swinderniana*, 15, 19, 203
   *swinderniana emini*, 203
   *swinderniana swinderniana*, 203
   *swinderniana zenkeri*, 203
   *taranta*, 15; 20; 206
Aviary, 28
   construction, 36
   covered section, 35
   electric lighting, 37; 38
   extra equipment, 38
   flight, the, 28
   floor, the, 106
   layout, 33
   maintenance, 41-43
   materials, 28-31
   open section, 33
   shape and size, 31
   shelter, the, 35
   shrubbery, 41
   ventilation, 36

Bath, 100; 104
Behavior, 10
   Abyssinian, 207; 211; 216
   Black-cheeked, 146
   Black-collared, 204; 205
   Fischer's 131
   Madagascar, 114; 115; 120; 121
   Masked, 150; 155; 156
   Nyasaland, 137
   Peach-faced, 178; 179; 186; 187
   Red-headed, 167; 170; 171

Bird-room, 39
   humidity, 39
Black-cheeked lovebird, 16; 23; 141
Black-collared lovebird, 15; 19; 203
Black-winged lovebird, 15; 20; 206
Blue-winged Dwarf Parrotlet, 203
Brazilian Blue-winged Dwarf Parrotlet, 226
Breeding, Abyssinian, 210; 212; 213
   Black-cheeked, 143
   Black-collared, 205
   Fischer's, 127; 131; 132
   Madagascar, 115; 116; 121; 122
   Masked, 153; 154; 155
   minerals, importance of, 45
   Nyasaland, 138; 139
   Peach-faced, 190; 191
   premature, 62
   Red-headed, 160; 162
   time, 62

Ceara Dwarf Parrotlet, 226
Celestial Parrotlet, 222
Ceylon Hanging Parrot, 241
Chromosomal karyotype, 82
Cloaca, examination of, 82
Color mutations, Abyssinian, 217
   Fischer's 133
   Masked, 158-158
   Madagascar, 124
   Nyasaland, 140
   Peach-faced, 198-202
   Red-headed, 171
Colors of lovebirds
   Abyssinian, 206; 207
   Black-cheeked, 141
   Black-collared, 203; 204
   Fischer's, 124; 125
   Masked, 147
   Madagascar, 113
   Nyasaland, 135
   Peach-faced, 175
   Red-headed, 159
Coxen's Lorilet, 249

Courting, Peach-faced, 194
  Masked, 153
Cross-breeding, 10; 12; 13; 25; 27
  Peach-faced, 197
Cuttlebone, 97

Death-in-shell, 59; 62
Delicate Parrotlet, 227
Distribution of lovebirds, 9
  Abyssinian, 208
  Black-cheeked, 144
  Black-collared, 203
  Fischer's, 126
  Madagascar, 112
  Masked, 147; 149
  Nyasaland, 135; 137
  Peach-faced, 175
  Red-headed, 159
Double-eyed Fig Parrot, 247; 248
Down color, 67
Drinking and bath water, 100

Egg-tooth, 59

Feather-picking, 129; 138; 190; 215
Feeders, 91; 94
Feeding of lovebirds, 10; 86
  Abyssinian, 215
  Black-cheeked, 143
  Black-collared, 204
  Fischer's, 126; 129
  fledglings, 70; 71
  Madagascar, 122
  Masked, 150; 151
  Nyasaland, 138; 139
  Red-headed, 170
  Peach-faced, 190; 191
Fischer's lovebird, 124
Flores Hanging Parrot, 242
*Forpus* species
  aviary behavior, 220
  feeding, 221
*Forpus*, 219
  *coelestis coelestis*, 222
  *xanthops*, 222
  *conspicillatus*, 236
  *cyanopygius*, 234
  *passerinus*, 226
  *passerinus crassicostris*, 230
  *passerinus cyanochlorus*, 229
  *passerinus cyanophanes*, 229
  *passerinus deliciousus*, 227
  *passerinus flavescens*, 232
  *passerinus flavissimus*, 226
  *passerinus olallae*, 226; 233
  *passerinus passerinus*, 227
  *passerinus vividus*, 230
  *passerinus spengeli*, 232
  *viridissimus*, 232
  *sclateri*, 236
Fruit, 95

Greens, 94
Golden-fronted Hanging Parrot, 243
Gray-headed lovebird, 15; 112
Grit, 97
Growth of chicks, 71
  Peach-faced, 182
Guiana Parrotlet, 226
Guyana Dwarf Parrotlet, 227
Gyldenstolpe's Parrotlet, 233

Hacha Dwarf Parrotlet, 229
Hanging Parrots, 239
Hartlaub's Dwarf Parrotlet, 229
Hatching of lovebirds, 58; 59
  History, 16-24
  Abyssinian, 214
  Black-cheeked, 145; 146
  Fischer's, 125
  Masked, 149
  Nyasaland, 135; 137
  Peach-faced, 186
  Red-headed, 163
Hybrids of lovebirds,
  Abyssinian, 217
  Black-cheeked, 146
  Fischer's, 133; 134
  Masked, 158
  Nyasaland, 140
  Peach-faced, 202

Illness, 106
  symptoms, 108; 110
  treatment, 109; 110; 112
Incubation period, 58; 59

Large-billed Parrotlet, 230
Lilian's lovebird, 135
*Loriculus*, 239
  *aurantiifrons*, 243
  *beryllimus*, 241
  *galgulus*, 241
  *pasillus*, 246
  *philippensis*, 244
  *stigmatus*, 244
  *vernalis*, 245

Madagascar lovebird, 15; 113
Marshall's lorilet, 248
Masked lovebird, 147
Mexican Parrotlet, 234

Moluccan Hanging Parrot, 243
Nest box, 44; 51; 52-54; 105
  access to, 46
  cleaning, 63
  construction, 51; 54
  entrance, 52
  humidity, 44; 105
  size specifications, 51-53
Nesting habits, Abyssinian, 208; 210; 212
  Black-cheeked, 143
  Fischer's, 131; 132
  Madagascar, 114; 115; 116
  Masked, 154; 155
  Nyasaland, 138; 139
  Peach-faced, 179; 182; 193; 194
  Red-headed, 160; 162
Nesting materials, 51; 104; 105
Nest inspections, 62
Nutrition, 24
Nyasaland lovebird, 135

*Opopsitta*
  *diophthalma diophthalma*, 247
  *diophthalma aurensis*, 248; 249
  *diophthalma coccinelfrons*, 247
  *diophthalma coxeni*, 247; 249
  *diophthalma festetichi*, 247
  *diophthalma inseparabilis*, 247
  *diophthalma macleayana*, 249
  *diophthalma marshalli*, 247
  *gulielmiterti amabilis*, 251
  *gulielmiterti fuscifrons*, 251
  *gulielmiterti melanogenia*, 250
  *gulielmiterti nigrifrons*, 251
  *gulielmiterti ramuensis*, 251
  *gulielmiterti suavissima*, 251

Orange-breasted Fig Parrot, 250
Ovulation, 57

Palaeornidae, 9
Peach-faced lovebird, 16; 21; 174
Pelvic-bone test, 75
Perches, 102-103
  installation of, 103

Philippine Hanging Parrot, 244
Psittacosis, 24

Ramsay's lorilet, 248
Rearing, hand, 67; 70; 71
  food, Fischer's, 129
Red-capped Hanging Parrot, 244
Red-faced lovebird, 15; 159
Red-headed lovebird, 15; 159
Ridgway's Blue-winged Dwarf Parrotlet, 230
Ringing birds, 46; 50; 66; 156
Rosefaced lovebird, 21; 174

Salvadori's Dwarf Parrotlet, 232
Sclater's Parrotlet, 236
Sandbath, 104
Seed, 87
  mixture, 94
Sexing lovebirds, 74-82
  Abyssinian, 74
  Black-cheeked, 74
  Madagascar, 74
  Nyasaland, 74
  Peach-faced, 74
  Red-headed, 74
Sex-steroids, ratio of, 82
Spectacled Parrotlet, 236
Spengel's Dwarf Parrotlet, 232
Swindern's lovebird, 19; 203

Taming
  Abyssinian, 212
  Madagascar, 119; 120
  Red-headed, 166; 167
Turquoise-rumped Parrotlet, 234

Venezuelan Green-rumped Parrotlet, 232
Vernal Hanging Parrot, 245
Vitamins, 138

Wing-clipping, 117; 166; 167

Yellow-collared lovebird, 147
Yellow-throated Hanging Parrot, 246